D0875844

PEACOCK

Memoirs of Shelley
and other Essays and Reviews

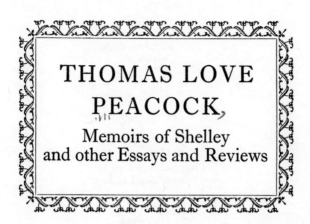

THOMAS LOVE PEACOCK,

Memoirs of Shelley
and other Essays and Reviews

Edited by
HOWARD MILLS

NEW YORK UNIVERSITY PRESS
NEW YORK 1970

© New York University Press 1970
First published 1970
Rupert Hart-Davis Ltd London

Library of Congress Card Number:
76 - 129 - 350

ISBN: 0-8147-5354-x

Printed in Great Britain

CONTENTS

FOREWORD

This book aims to make accessible the best of Peacock's essays and reviews which, with the exception of *The Four Ages of Poetry*, are not otherwise available outside the expensive reprint of the ten-volume Halliford Edition. It will form a companion volume to David Garnett's edition of Peacock's complete novels: but these essays are not simply of marginal interest as glosses on and parallels to the novels. They stand independently as critical accounts of the spirit of the age in general and particular important figures.

The major work, and the longest (which I have therefore moved out of the chronological sequence to the front of the book) is the *Memoirs of Shelley*. They were written forty years after the friendship, between 1858 and 1862, when Peacock was in his seventies, and are contemporary with his last novel *Gryll Grange*. In that novel the central character of Falconer, a compound ghost of the young Shelley and the young Peacock, is a poignantly remote, gentle, pastoral figure. But the Shelley of the Memoirs has all the vividness, disconcerting unpredictability and warmth we encounter in his letters—or in his recreation in *Nightmare Abbey*.

Contemporary with *Nightmare Abbey* (1818) is the *Essay on Fashionable Literature*, which characterizes the dullness (in the Popeian sense) and rigged reputations of the Edinburgh and Quarterly reviewers, and defends Coleridge's *Christabel*. Peacock planned to continue with a similar defence of *The Excursion*, but neither completed nor published the essay which remains virtually unknown compared with *The Four Ages of*

Poetry. The confident brilliance of the latter, written two years later in 1820 and utterly different in its viewpoint, comes from Peacock's growing impatience with Shelley's poetry and more so with his own, and his self-congratulation at having landed a post of 'utility' at East India House after uneasy years as a leisured littérateur. The essay would have been more fruitful if this overbearing self-confidence had been checked by Peacock feeling the need to distinguish between Wordsworth or Shelley and Campbell or Moore, or the need to answer, say, Wordsworth's *Essay Supplementary to the Preface of 1815* or (by a reversal of the actual order) Shelley's *Defence of Poetry*. As it was, Peacock set Shelley too low and rickety a hurdle.

If *The Four Ages* is wilfully reductive, it is surely to Peacock's credit in his review of Moore's life of Byron in 1830 to reduce Byron to the ordinary and undistinguished. He perceived, at a time when Byron was still seen as a titanic figure, the paradox Arnold later expressed in his essay on Heine: Byron 'was eminent only by his genius, by his inborn force and fire...except for his genius he was an ordinary nineteenth-century English gentleman with little culture and no ideas'. Peacock's target is equally the cant and flash style of Moore: while Peacock passingly defends Byron from his friend, the general effect is to suggest that they richly deserved each other. To expose Moore's cant about irreligion Peacock quotes from Thomas Jefferson, whose Memoirs, Correspondence and Private Papers he reviewed in the same year (1830). From this review, which in turn makes a glancing attack on 'the soul-withering influence of our own frivolous and sycophantic literature', I have reprinted the strikingly enthusiastic passages which may surprise those who know Peacock only from his novels and who take the views on America of Dr Opimiam in *Gryll Grange* to be the author's own.

But the readers of the novels will not be surprised that in the early 1830's Peacock regularly reviewed opera and other concerts for *The Globe* and *The Examiner*. The three I have reprinted for their intrinsic critical interest do not do enough justice to his range of subject but the review of Mount Edg-

cumbe's *Musical Reminiscences,* here reprinted in full, gave him
the opportunity to survey the whole history of opera in England
and distinguish his own intelligent conservatism from Edgcumbe's self-confessedly reactionary preference for 'the good
old style'. In the more general passages of the article written
after Bellini's death Peacock develops his criteria of 'expression'
and 'simplicity' and his conviction, reminiscent of the end of
Johnson's *Life of Gray,* that 'the feelings of the ordinary unsophisticated and unprejudiced hearer are always in advance of
their rules (musical critics'); and that which has, in despite of
them, been once stamped with popular favour, becomes a
standard to the same class of critics of the next generation.'

A less optimistic view of the taste of the period emerges from
the essays on *French Comic Romances* and the *Épicier.* The
opening of the first has often been quoted for its discussion of
satire and comedy and its obvious relevance to Peacock's own
novels: less well known is the close, with its comments on the
spirit of the age which lead into the analysis of the grocer or
shopkeeper mentality in the second essay.

The Last Day of Windsor Forest (*c.* 1862) is perhaps the last
thing Peacock wrote: he died before seeing it through the press.
It came from the frank nostalgia which produced much of *Gryll
Grange* and which, he says, 'seems inseparable from old age'. A
sign that we have moved through this volume from the 1810's
to the 1860's is that the once revolutionary poet whom Peacock
defended in his first essay has in this last essay become absorbed
into a classical taste as an established spokesman for mankind's
great and recurrent feelings. This essay, like *Gryll Grange,*
constantly turns to Wordsworth as someone an old man has
come to rely on, in Johnson's Wordsworthian phrase, 'to awaken
those ideas that slumber in the heart'.

Like most editors of selections I have been harassed by the
problem of priorities for the allowed space. A first decision was
to include complete five major pieces: *Memoirs of Shelley, An
Essay on Fashionable Literature, The Four Ages of Poetry, Mount
Edgcumbe's Musical Reminiscences* and *The Épicier.* The short

articles on *Paganini* and *Windsor Forest* are also complete. Reprinted with minor cuts of Peacock's over-indulgent quotation and paraphrase is *Moore's Byron*: the reviews of Mozart and Beethoven are also virtually complete (the unreprinted close of the latter changes the subject to Italian opera). From the other essays I have taken the sections of general and lasting interest, indicating cuts clearly and on occasion describing the omitted section. The reader keen to look up the rest of Peacock's essays will find, in the Halliford Edition, *Moore's Epicurean* (1827), *Chronicles of London Bridge* (1830), *The Legend of Manor Hall* and *Recollections of Childhood: The Abbey House* (1837), *Gastronomy and Civilization* (with his daughter) (1851), *Horae Dramaticae* (1852 and 1857), *Müller and Donaldson's History of Greek Literature* (1859) and *Unpublished Letters of Percy Bysshe Shelley. From Italy—1818 to 1822* (letters to Peacock reprinted with a short introduction in Fraser's Magazine, March 1860). The first of these—the only one with a strong claim to be reprinted—was finally put aside because of the luxurious length of its sarcastic paraphrasing. Of its two general arguments one, the exposure of Moore's false imagery, repeats too closely the work done in the review of Moore's *Byron*, and the other, the bizarre approximation of the Epicurean and Benthamite philosophies, is much too short to pull out of its context.

The essays in this selection first appeared as follows:

An Essay on Fashionable Literature first published complete in the Halliford Edition.

The Four Ages of Poetry in Olliers Literary Miscellany no. 1, 1820.

Moore's Letters & Journals of Lord Byron, vol. 1 in Westminster Review, vol. XII; Apr. 1830.

Memoirs, Correspondence and Private Papers of Thomas Jefferson in Westminster Review, vol. XIII; Oct. 1830.

Paganini in The Examiner, 12 June 1831.

Beethoven in The Examiner, 27 May 1832.

Mozart in The Examiner, 2 June 1833.

Lord Mount Edgcumbe's Musical Reminiscences in The London Review, vol. 1; Apr. 1835.

French Comic Romances in The London Review, vol. II; Oct. 1836.

The Épicier in The London Review, vol. II; Jan. 1836.

Bellini in the same number of The London Review.

Memoirs of Percy Bysshe Shelley in Fraser's Magazine, June 1858.

Memoirs of Shelley (second paper) in Fraser's Magazine, Jan. 1860.

Percy Bysshe Shelley. Supplementary Notice in Fraser's Magazine, March 1862.

The Last Day of Windsor Forest first published by Richard Garnett in the National Review, Sept. 1887.

These texts are reproduced here as they appear with minor corrections in vols. 8 to 10 of the Halliford Edition of Peacock's Works, ed. H. F. B. Brett-Smith and C. E. Jones, London 1924–34 (reprinted New York 1967). The only exception is the review of Beethoven of which the Halliford editors print one paragraph: I have taken this article direct from The Examiner.

Unless otherwise indicated, the footnotes are Peacock's own.

The following discuss Peacock's essays and reviews:

H. F. B. Brett-Smith (ed.), *Peacock's Four Ages of Poetry, Shelley's Defence of Poetry* (etc.), Oxford 1921.

Carl Dawson, *His Fine Wit*, London 1970.

E. D. MacKerness, 'Peacock's Musical Criticism' in *The Wind and the Rain*, vol. 4, no. 3, 1948.

J.-J. Mayoux, *Un Épicurean Anglais: Thomas Love Peacock*, Paris 1933.

Howard Mills, *Peacock: his Circle and his Age*, London 1969.

MEMOIRS OF
PERCY BYSSHE
SHELLEY

MEMOIRS OF
PERCY BYSSHE SHELLEY*

Rousseau, ne recevant aucun auteur, remercie Madame———de ses bontés, et la prie de ne plus venir chez lui.

ROUSSEAU had a great aversion to visitors of all classes, but especially to literary visitors, feeling sure that they would print something about him. A lady who had long persisted in calling on him, one day published a *brochure*, and sent him a copy. He rejoiced in the opportunity which brought her under his rule of exclusion, and terminated their intercourse by the above *billet-doux*.

Rousseau's rule bids fair to become general with all who wish to keep in the *secretum iter et fallentis semita vitæ*, and not to become materials for general gossip. For not only is a departed author of any note considered a fair subject to be dissected at the tea-table of the reading public, but all his friends and connexions, however quiet and retiring and unobtrusive may have been the general tenor of their lives, must be served up with him. It is the old village scandal on a larger scale; and as in these days of universal locomotion people know nothing of their neighbours, they prefer tittle-tattle about notorieties to the retailing of whispers about the Jenkinses and Tomkinses of the vicinity.

---

* *Shelley and his Writings.* By Charles S. Middleton. London: Newby 1858. *Recollections of the Last Days of Shelley and Byron.* By E. J. Trelawny. London: Moxon 1858. *The Life of Percy Bysshe Shelley.* By Thomas Jefferson Hogg. In Four Volumes. Vols. 1 and 2. London: Moxon 1858.

This appetite for gossip about notorieties being once created in the 'reading public', there will be always found persons to minister to it; and among the volunteers of this service, those who are best informed and who most valued the departed will probably not be the foremost. Then come biographies abounding with errors; and then, as matter of defence perhaps, comes on the part of friends a tardy and more authentic narrative. This is at best, as Mr Hogg describes it, a 'difficult and delicate task'. But it is always a matter of choice and discretion. No man is bound to write the life of another. No man who does so is bound to tell the public all he knows. On the contrary, he is bound to keep to himself whatever may injure the interests or hurt the feelings of the living, especially when the latter have in no way injured or calumniated the dead, and are not necessarily brought before the tribunal of public opinion in the character of either plaintiffs or defendants. Neither if there be in the life of the subject of the biography any event which he himself would willingly have blotted from the tablet of his own memory, can it possibly be the duty of a survivor to drag it into daylight. If such an event be the cardinal point of a life; if to conceal it or to misrepresent it would be to render the whole narrative incomplete, incoherent, unsatisfactory alike to the honour of the dead and the feelings of the living; then, as there is no moral compulsion to speak of the matter at all, it is better to let the whole story slumber in silence.

Having lived some years in very familiar intimacy with the subject of these memoirs; having had as good opportunities as any, and better than most persons now living, to observe and appreciate his great genius, extensive acquirements, cordial friendships, disinterested devotion to the well-being of the few with whom he lived in domestic intercourse, and ardent endeavours by private charity and public advocacy to ameliorate the condition of the many who pass their days in unremunerating toil; having been named his executor conjointly with Lord Byron, whose death, occurring before that of Shelley's father, when the son's will came into effect, left me alone in that capacity; having lived after his death in the same cordial intimacy with his widow, her family, and one or two at least of his surviving friends, I have been considered to have some peculiar advantages for writing his life, and have often been requested to do so; but for the reasons above given I have always refused.

Wordsworth says to the Cuckoo:

> O blithe new-comer! I have heard,
>   I hear thee, and rejoice.
> O Cuckoo! shall I call thee Bird,
>   Or but a wandering Voice?
>
> *   *   *
>
> Thrice welcome, darling of the Spring!
>   Even yet thou art to me
> No bird, but an invisible thing,
>   A voice, a mystery.

Shelley was fond of repeating these verses, and perhaps they were not forgotten in his poem *To a Skylark*:

> Hail to thee, blithe spirit!
>   Bird thou never wert,
> That from heaven, or near it,
>   Pourest thy full heart,
> In profuse strains of unpremeditated art.
>
> *   *   *
>
> The pale purple even
>   Melts around thy flight:
> Like a star of heaven,
>   In the broad daylight,
> Thou art unseen, but yet I hear thy shrill delight.

Now, I could have wished that, like Wordsworth's Cuckoo, he had been allowed to remain a voice and a mystery: that, like his own Skylark, he had been left unseen in his congenial region,

> Above the smoke and stir of this dim spot
> Which men call earth,

and that he had been only heard in the splendour of his song. But since it is not to be so, since so much has been, and so much more will probably be, written about him, the motives which deterred me from originating a substantive work on the subject, do not restrict me from commenting on what has been published by others, and from correcting errors, if such should appear to me to occur, in the narratives which I may pass under review.

I have placed the works at the head of this article in the order in which they were published. I have no acquaintance with Mr Middleton. Mr Trelawny and Mr Hogg I may call my friends.

Mr Middleton's work is chiefly a compilation from previous publications, with some very little original matter, curiously obtained.

Mr Trelawny's work relates only to the later days of Mr Shelley's life in Italy.

Mr Hogg's work is the result of his own personal knowledge, and of some inedited letters and other documents, either addressed to himself or placed at his disposal by Sir Percy Shelley and his lady. It is to consist of four volumes, of which the two just published bring down the narrative to the period immediately preceding Shelley's separation from his first wife. At that point I shall terminate this first part of my proposed review.

I shall not anticipate opinions, but shall go over all that is important in the story as briefly as I can, interspersing such observations as may suggest themselves in its progress.

Percy Bysshe Shelley was born at his father's seat, Field Place, in Sussex, on the 4th of August 1792. His grandfather, Sir Bysshe Shelley, was then living, and his father, Timothy Shelley, Esquire, was then or subsequently a Member of Parliament. The family was of great antiquity; but Percy conferred more honour on it than he derived from it.

He had four sisters and a brother, the youngest of the family, and the days of his childhood appear to have passed affectionately in his domestic society.

To the first ten years of his life we have no direct testimony but that of his sister Hellen, in a series of letters to Lady Shelley, published in the beginning of Mr Hogg's work. In the first of these she says:

> A child who at six years old was sent daily to learn Latin at a clergyman's house, and as soon as it was expedient removed to Dr Greenland's, from thence to Eton, and subsequently to college, could scarcely have been the *uneducated* son that some writers would endeavour to persuade those who read their books to believe he ought to have been, if his parents despised education.

Miss Hellen gives an illustration of Shelley's boyish traits of imagination:

> On one occasion he gave the most minute details of a visit he had paid to some ladies with whom he was acquainted at our village. He described their reception of him, their occupations, and the wandering in their pretty garden, where there was a well-remembered filbert-walk and an undulating turf-bank, the delight of our morning visit. There must have been something peculiar in this little event; for I have often heard it mentioned as a singular fact, and it was ascertained almost immediately, that the boy had never been to the house. It was not considered as a falsehood to be punished; but I imagine his conduct altogether must have been so little understood and unlike that of the generality of children, that these tales were left unnoticed.

Mr Hogg says at a later date:

> He was altogether incapable of rendering an account of any transaction whatsoever, according to the strict and precise truth, and the bare naked realities of actual life; not through an addiction to falsehood, which he cordially detested, but because he was the creature, the unsuspecting and unresisting victim, of his irresistible imagination.
>
> Had he written to ten different individuals the history of some proceeding in which he was himself a party and an eye-witness, each of his ten reports would have varied from the rest in essential and important circumstances. The relation given on the morrow would be unlike that of the day, as the latter would contradict the tale of yesterday.

Several instances will be given of the habit, thus early developed in Shelley, of narrating, as real, events which had never occurred; and his friends and relations have thought it necessary to give

prominence to this habit as a characteristic of his strong imagi-
nativeness predominating over reality. Coleridge has written
much and learnedly on this subject of ideas with the force of
sensations, of which he found many examples in himself.

At the age of ten, Shelley was sent to Sion House Academy,
near Brentford. 'Our master,' says his schoolfellow, Captain
Medwin, 'a Scotch Doctor of Law, and a divine, was a choleric
man, of a sanguinary complexion, in a green old age, not wanting in good qualities, but very capricious in his temper, which,
good or bad, was influenced by the daily occurrences of a
domestic life not the most harmonious, and of which his face
was the barometer and his hand the index.' This worthy was
in the habit of cracking unbecoming jokes, at which most of the
boys laughed; but Shelley, who could not endure this sort of
pleasantry, received them with signs of aversion. A day or two
after one of these exhibitions, when Shelley's manifestation of
dislike to the matter had attracted the preceptor's notice,
Shelley had a theme set him for two Latin lines on the subject
of *Tempestas*.

> He came to me (says Medwin) to assist him in the task. I had a
> cribbing book, of which I made great use, Ovid's *Tristibus*. I knew
> that the only work of Ovid with which the Doctor was acquainted
> was the *Metamorphoses*, and by what I thought good luck, I hap-
> pened to stumble on two lines exactly applicable to the purpose.
> The hexameter I forgot, but the pentameter ran thus: *Jam, jam
> tacturos sidera celsa putes.*

So far the story is not very classically told. The title of the book
should have been given as *Tristia*, or *De Tristibus*; and the reading is *tacturas*, not *tacturos*; *summa*, not *celsa*: the latter term is
inapplicable to the stars. The distich is this:

> *Me miserum! quanti montes volvuntur aquarum!*
> *Jam, jam tacturas sidera summa putes.*

Something was probably substituted for *Me miserum!* But be
this as it may, Shelley was grievously beaten for what the school-

master thought bad Latin.* The Doctor's judgment was of a piece with that of the Edinburgh Reviewers, when taking a line of Pindar, which Payne Knight had borrowed in a Greek translation 'of a passage in Gray's *Bard*, to have been Payne Knight's own, they pronounced it to be nonsense.†

The name of the Brentford Doctor according to Miss Hellen Shelley was Greenland, and according to Mr Hogg it was Greenlaw. Captain Medwin does not mention the name, but says, 'So much did we mutually hate Sion House, that we never alluded to it in after life.' Mr Hogg says, 'In walking with Shelley to Bishopsgate‡ from London, he pointed out to me more than once a gloomy brick house as being this school. He spoke of the master, Doctor Greenlaw, not without respect, saying, "he was a hard-headed Scotchman, and a man of rather liberal opinions".' Of this period of his life he never gave me an account, nor have I heard or read any details which appeared to bear the impress of truth. Between these two accounts the Doctor and his character seem reduced to a myth. I myself know nothing of the matter. I do not remember Shelley ever mentioning the Doctor to me. But we shall find as we proceed, that when ever there are two evidences to one transaction, many

---

* Not for the erroneous use of *celsa*, but for the true Ovidian Latin, which the Doctor held to be bad.

† θερμὰ δ' ὁ τέγγων δάκρυα στοναχαῖς. This line, which a synod of North British critics has peremptorily pronounced to be nonsense, is taken from the tenth Nemean of Pindar, v. 141; and until they passed sentence upon it in No. XIV. of the *Edinburgh Review*, was universally thought to express with peculiar force and delicacy the mixture of indignation and tenderness so appropriate to the grief of the hero of the modern as well as of the ancient ode. (*Principles of Taste*, Part II. c. 2.)

I imagine there are many verses in the best classical poets which, if presented as original, would not pass muster with either teachers or critics.

‡ More properly Bishopgate, without the s: the entrance to Windsor Park from Englefield Green. Shelley had a furnished house, in 1815–16, very near to this park gate.

of the recorded events of Shelley's life will resolve themselves
into the same mythical character.

At the best, Sion House Academy must have been a bad
beginning of scholastic education for a sensitive and imaginative
boy.

After leaving this academy, he was sent, in his fifteenth year,
to Eton. The head master was Doctor Keate, a less mythical
personage than the Brentford Orbilius, but a variety of the same
genus. Mr Hogg says:

> Dr Keate was a short, short-necked, short-legged, man – thick-
> set, powerful, and very active. His countenance resembled that of
> a bull-dog; the expression was not less sweet and bewitching: his
> eyes, his nose, and especially his mouth, were exactly like that
> comely and engaging animal, and so were his short crooked legs.
> It was said in the school that old Keate could pin and hold a bull
> with his teeth. His iron sway was the more unpleasant and shock-
> ing after the long mild Saturnian reign of Dr Goodall, whose
> temper, character, and conduct corresponded precisely with his
> name, and under whom Keate had been master of the lower
> school. Discipline, wholesome and necessary in moderation, was
> carried by him to an excess. It is reported that on one morning he
> flogged eighty boys. Although he was rigid, coarse, and despotical,
> some affirm that on the whole he was not unjust, nor altogether
> devoid of kindness. His behaviour was accounted vulgar and un-
> gentlemanlike, and therefore he was particularly odious to the
> gentlemen of the school, especially to the refined and aristocratical
> Shelley.

But Shelley suffered even more from his school-fellows than he
did from his master. It had been so at Brentford, and it was still
more so at Eton, from the more organized system of fagging, to
which no ill-usage would induce him to submit. But among his
equals in age he had several attached friends, and one of these,
in a letter dated February 27th, 1857, gives the following
reminiscences of their Eton days: (Hogg, i. 43.)

> MY DEAR MADAM, – Your letter has taken me back to the sunny
> time of boyhood, 'when thought is speech and speech is truth,'
> when I was the friend and companion of Shelley at Eton. What
> brought us together in that small world was, I suppose, kindred

feelings, and the predominance of fancy and imagination. Many a long and happy walk have I had with him in the beautiful neighbourhood of dear old Eton. We used to wander for hours about Clewer, Frogmore, the park at Windsor, the Terrace; and I was a delighted and willing listener to his marvellous stories of fairyland, and apparitions, and spirits, and haunted ground; and his speculations were then (for his mind was far more developed than mine) of the world beyond the grave. Another of his favourite rambles was Stoke Park, and the picturesque churchyard where Gray is said to have written his *Elegy*, of which he was very fond. I was myself far too young to form any estimate of character, but I loved Shelley for his kindliness and affectionate ways. He was not made to endure the rough and boisterous pastime at Eton, and his shy and gentle nature was glad to escape far away, to muse over strange fancies, for his mind was reflective and teeming with deep thought. His lessons were child's play to him, and his power of Latin versification marvellous. I think I remember some long work he had even then commenced, but I never saw it. His love of nature was intense, and the sparkling poetry of his mind shone out of his speaking eye when he was dwelling on anything good or great. He certainly was not happy at Eton, for his was a disposition that needed especial personal superintendence to watch and cherish and direct all his noble aspirations and the remarkable tenderness of his heart. He had great moral courage, and feared nothing but what was base, and false, and low. He never joined in the usual sports of the boys, and what is remarkable, never went out in a boat on the river. What I have here set down will be of little use to you, but will please you as a sincere and truthful and humble tribute to one whose good name was sadly whispered away. Shelley said to me when leaving Oxford under a cloud, 'Halliday, I am come to say good-bye to you, if you are not afraid to be seen with me!' I saw him once again in the autumn of 1814, when he was glad to introduce me to his wife. I think he said he was just come from Ireland. You have done quite right in applying to me direct, and I am only sorry that I have no anecdotes or letters of that period to furnish.

I am, yours truly,

WALTER S. HALLIDAY.

This is the only direct testimony to Shelley's Eton life from one who knew him there. It contains two instances of how little value can be attached to any other than such direct testimony. That at that time he never went out in a boat on the river I believe to be strictly true; nevertheless Captain Medwin says: 'He told me the greatest delight he experienced at Eton was from boating…He never lost the fondness with which he regarded the Thames, no new acquaintance when he went to Eton, for at Brentford we had more than once played the truant, and rowed to Kew, and once to Richmond.' But these truant excursions were exceptional. His affection for boating began at a much later period, as I shall have occasion to notice. The second instance is: 'I think he said he was just come from Ireland.' In the autumn of 1814 it was not from Ireland, but from the Continent that he had just returned,

Captain Medwin's *Life of Shelley* abounds with inaccuracies; not intentional misrepresentations, but misapprehensions and errors of memory. Several of these occur in reference to Shelley's boyish passion for his cousin Harriet Grove. This, like Lord Byron's early love for Miss Chaworth, came to nothing. But most boys of any feeling and imagination have some such passion, and, as in these instances, it usually comes to nothing. Much more has been made of both these affairs than they are worth. It is probable that few of Johnson's poets passed through their boyhood without a similar attachment, but if it came at all under the notice of our literary Hercules, he did not think it worth recording. I shall notice this love-affair in its proper place, but chiefly for the sake of separating from it one or two matters which have been erroneously assigned to it.

Shelley often spoke to me of Eton, and of the persecutions he had endured from the elder boys, with feelings of abhorrence which I never heard him express in an equal degree in relation to any other subject, except when he spoke of Lord Chancellor Eldon. He told me that he had been provoked into striking a penknife through the hand of one of his young tyrants, and pinning it to the desk, and that this was the cause of his leaving Eton prematurely: but his imagination often presented past events to him as they might have been, not as they were. Such a circumstance must have been remembered by others if it had actually occurred. But if the occurrence was imaginary, it was in a memory of cordial detestation that the imagination arose.

Mr Hogg vindicates the system of fagging, and thinks he was himself the better for the discipline in after life. But Mr Hogg is a man of imperturbable temper and adamantine patience: and with all this he may have fallen into good hands, for all big boys are not ruffians. But Shelley was a subject totally unfit for the practice in its best form, and he seems to have experienced it in its worst.

At Eton he became intimate with Doctor Lind, 'a name well known among the professors of medical science', says Mrs Shelley, who proceeds:

'This man,' Shelley has often said, 'is exactly what an old man ought to be. Free, calm-spirited, full of benevolence, and even of youthful ardour; his eye seemed to burn with supernatural spirit beneath his brow, shaded by his venerable white locks; he was tall, vigorous, and healthy in his body, tempered, as it had ever been, by his amiable mind. I owe to that man far, ah! far more than I owe to my father; he loved me, and I shall never forget our long talks, when he breathed the spirit of the kindest tolerance and the purest wisdom. Once, when I was very ill during the holidays, as I was recovering from a fever which had attacked my brain, a servant overheard my father consult about sending me to a private madhouse. I was a favourite among all our servants, so this fellow came and told me, as I lay sick in bed. My horror was beyond words, and I might soon have been mad indeed if they had proceeded in their iniquitous plan. I had one hope. I was master of three pounds in money, and with the servant's help I contrived to send an express to Dr Lind. He came, and I shall never forget his manner on that occasion. His profession gave him authority; his love for me ardour. He dared my father to execute his purpose, and his menaces had the desired effect.'

Mr Hogg subjoins:

I have heard Shelley speak of his fever, and this scene at Field Place, more than once, in nearly the same terms as Mrs Shelley adopts. It appeared to myself, and to others also, that his recollections were those of a person not quite recovered from a fever, and still disturbed by the horrors of the disease.

However this may have been, the idea that his father was continually on the watch for a pretext to lock him up, haunted him through life, and a mysterious intimation of his father's intention to effect such a purpose was frequently received by him, and communicated to his friends as a demonstration of the necessity under which he was placed of changing his residence and going abroad.

I pass over his boyish schemes for raising the devil, of which much is said in Mr Hogg's book. He often spoke of them to me; but the principal fact of which I have any recollection was one which he treated only as a subject of laughter—the upsetting into the fire in his chamber at Eton of a frying-pan full of diabolical ingredients, and the rousing up all the inmates in his dame's house in the dead of the night by the abominable effluvia. If he had ever had any faith in the possible success of his incantations, he had lost if before I knew him.

We now come to the first really important event of his life—his expulsion from Oxford.

At University College, Oxford, in October, 1810, Mr Hogg first became acquainted with him. In their first conversation Shelley was exalting the physical sciences, especially chemistry. Mr Hogg says:

> As I felt but little interest in the subject of his conversation, I had leisure to examine, and I may add to admire, the appearance of my very extraordinary guest. It was a sum of many contradictions. His figure was slight and fragile, and yet his bones and joints were large and strong. He was tall, but he stooped so much that he seemed of a low stature. His clothes were expensive, and made according to the most approved mode of the day; but they were tumbled, rumpled, unbrushed. His gestures were abrupt and sometimes violent, occasionally even awkward, yet more frequently gentle and graceful. His complexion was delicate and almost feminine, of the purest white and red; yet he was tanned and freckled by exposure to the sun...His features, his whole face, and particularly his head, were in fact unusually small; yet the last *appeared* of a remarkable bulk, for his hair was long and bushy...he often rubbed it up fiercely with his hands, or passed his fingers through his locks unconsciously, so that it was singularly wild and rough.

...His features were not symmetrical (the mouth perhaps excepted); yet was the effect of the whole extremely powerful. They breathed an animation, a fire, an enthusiasm, a vivid and preternatural intelligence, that I never met with in any other countenance. Nor was the moral expression less beautiful than the intellectual...I admired the enthusiasm of my new acquaintance, his ardour in the cause of science, and his thirst for knowledge. But there was one physical blemish that threatened to neutralize all his excellence.

This blemish was his voice.

There is a good deal in these volumes about Shelley's discordant voice. This defect he certainly had; but it was chiefly observable when he spoke under excitement. Then his voice was not only dissonant, like a jarring string, but he spoke in sharp fourths, the most unpleasing sequence of sound that can fall on the human ear: but it was scarcely so when he spoke calmly, and not at all so when he read; on the contrary, he seemed then to have his voice under perfect command: it was good both in tune and in tone; it was low and soft, but clear, distinct, and expressive. I have heard him read almost all Shakespeare's tragedies, and some of his more poetical comedies, and it was a pleasure to hear him read them.

Mr Hogg's description of Shelley's personal appearance gives a better idea of him than the portrait prefixed to his work, which is similar to that prefixed to the work of Mr Trelawny, except that Mr Trelawny's is lithographed* and Mr Hogg's is

---

* Mr Trelawny says, 'With reference to the likeness of Shelley in this volume, I must add, that he never sat to a professional artist. In 1819, at Rome, a daughter of the celebrated Curran began a portrait of him in oil, which she never finished, and left in an altogether flat and inanimate state. In 1821 or 1822, his friend Williams made a spirited water-colour drawing, which gave a very good idea of the poet. Out of these materials Mrs Williams, on her return to England after the death of Shelley, got Clint to compose a portrait, which the few who knew Shelley in the last year of his life thought very like him. The water-colour drawing has been lost, so that the portrait done by Clint is the only one of any value. I have had it copied and lithographed by Mr Vinter, an artist distinguished both for the fidelity and refinement of his works, and it is now published for the first time.'

engraved. These portraits do not impress themselves on me as likenesses. They seem to me to want the true outline of Shelley's features, and above all, to want their true expression. There is a portrait in the Florentine Gallery which represents him to me much more truthfully. It is that of Antonio Leisman, No. 155 of the *Ritratti de' Pittori*, in the Paris republication.

The two friends had made together a careful analysis of the doctrines of Hume. The papers were in Shelley's custody, and from a small part of them he made a little book, which he had printed, and which he sent by post to such persons as he thought would be willing to enter into a metaphysical discussion. He sent it under an assumed name, with a note, requesting that if the recipient were willing to answer the tract, the answer should be sent to a specified address in London. He received many answers; but in due time the little work and its supposed authors were denounced to the college authorities.

It was a fine spring morning, on Lady-day, in the year 1811 (says Mr Hogg), when I went to Shelley's rooms. He was absent; but before I had collected our books he rushed in. He was terribly agitated. I anxiously inquired what had happened.

'I am expelled,' he said, as soon as he had recovered himself a little. 'I am expelled! I was sent for suddenly a few minutes ago; I went to the common room, where I found our master, and two or three of the fellows. The master produced a copy of the little syllabus, and asked me if I were the author of it. He spoke in a rude, abrupt, and insolent tone. I begged to be informed for what purpose he put the question. No answer was given; but the master loudly and angrily repeated, "Are you the author of this book?" "If I can judge from your manner," I said, "you are resolved to punish me if I should acknowledge that it is my work. If you can prove that it is, produce your evidence; it is neither just nor lawful to interrogate me in such a case and for such a purpose. Such proceedings would become a court of inquisitors, but not free men in a free country." "Do you choose to deny that this is your composition?" the master reiterated in the same rude and angry voice.'

Shelley complained much of his violent and ungentlemanlike deportment, saying, 'I have experienced tyranny and injustice before, and I well know what vulgar violence is, but I never met with such unworthy treatment. I told him calmly but firmly that I was determined not to answer any questions respecting the publication on the table.

'He immediately repeated his demand; I persisted in my refusal. And he said furiously, "Then you are expelled; and I desire you will quit the college early to-morrow morning at the latest."

'One of the fellows took up two papers, and handed one of them to me; here it is.' He produced a regular sentence of expulsion, drawn up in due form, under the seal of the college. Shelley was full of spirit and courage, frank and fearless; but he was likewise shy, unpresuming, and eminently sensitive. I have been with him in many trying situations of his after-life, but I never saw him so deeply shocked and so cruelly agitated as on this occasion.

A nice sense of honour shrinks from the most distant touch of disgrace—even from the insults of those men whose contumely can bring no shame. He sat on the sofa, repeating with convulsive vehemence the words, 'Expelled, expelled!' his head shaking with emotion, and his whole frame quivering.

A similar scene followed with Mr Hogg himself, which he very graphically describes. The same questions, the same refusal to answer them, the same sentence of expulsion, and a peremptory order to quit the college early on the morrow. And accordingly, early on the next morning, Shelley and his friend took their departure from Oxford.

I accept Mr Hogg's account of this transaction as substantially correct. In Shelley's account of it to me there were material differences; and making all allowance for the degree in which, as already noticed, his imagination coloured the past, there is one matter of fact which remains inexplicable. According to him, his expulsion was a matter of great form and solemnity; there was a sort of public assembly, before which he pleaded his own cause, in a long oration, in the course of which he called on the illustrious spirits who had shed glory on those walls to look down on their degenerate successors. Now, the inexplicable matter to which I have alluded is this; he showed me an Oxford newspaper, containing a full report of the proceedings, with his own oration at great length. I suppose the pages of that diurnal were not deathless,* and that it would now be vain to search for it; but that he had it, and showed it to me, is absolutely certain. His oration may have been, as some of Cicero's published orations were, a speech in the potential mood; one which might, could, should, or would, have been spoken: but how in that case it got into the Oxford newspaper passes conjecture.

His expulsion from Oxford brought to a summary conclusion his boyish passion for Miss Harriet Grove. She would have no more to say to him; but I cannot see from his own letters, and those of Miss Hellen Shelley, that there had ever been much love on her side; neither can I find any reason to believe that it continued long on his. Mr Middleton follows Captain Medwin, who was determined that on Shelley's part it should be an enduring passion, and pressed into its service as testimonies some matters which had nothing to do with it. He says *Queen Mab* was dedicated to Harriet Grove, whereas it was certainly dedicated to Harriet Shelley; he even prints the dedication with the title 'To Harriet G.', whereas in the original the name of Harriet is only followed by asterisks; and of another little poem, he says, 'That Shelley's disappointment in love affected him acutely, may be seen by some lines inscribed erroneously "On F. G." instead of "H. G.", and doubtless of a much earlier date than assigned by Mrs Shelley to the fragment.' Now, I know the circumstances to which the fragment refers. The initials of the lady's name were F. G., and the date assigned to the fragment, 1817, was strictly correct. The intrinsic evidence of both poems will show their utter inapplicability to Miss Harriet Grove.

First let us see what Shelley himself says of her, in letters to Mr Hogg:

---

* Registered to fame eternal
In deathless pages of diurnal.
Hudibras.

Dec. 23, 1810.—Her disposition was in all probability divested of the enthusiasm by which mine is characterized...My sister attempted sometimes to plead my cause, but unsuccessfully. She said: 'Even supposing I take your representation of your brother's qualities and sentiments, which, as you coincide in and admire, I may fairly imagine to be exaggerated, although you may not be aware of the exaggeration, what right have I, admitting that he is so superior, to enter into an intimacy which must end in delusive disappointment when he finds how really inferior I am to the being his heated imagination has pictured?'

Dec. 26, 1810.—Circumstances have operated in such a manner that the attainment of the object of my heart was impossible, whether on account of extraneous influences, or from a feeling which possessed her mind, which told her not to deceive another, not to give him the possibility of disappointment.

Jan. 3, 1811.—She is no longer mine. She abhors me as a sceptic, as what she was before.

Jan. 11, 1811.—She is gone. She is lost to me for ever. She is married—married to a clod of earth. She will become as insensible herself: all those fine capabilities will moulder.

Next let us see what Miss Hellen Shelley says of the matter:

His disappointment in losing the lady of his love had a great effect upon him....It was not put an end to by *mutual* consent; but both parties were very young, and her father did not think the marriage would be for his daughter's happiness. He, however, with truly honourable feeling, would not have persisted in his objection if his daughter had considered herself bound by a promise to my brother; but this was not the case, and time healed the wound by means of another Harriet, whose name and similar complexion perhaps attracted the attention of my brother.

And lastly, let us see what the young lady's brother (C. H. G.) says of it:

After our visit at Field Place (in the year 1810), we went to my brother's house in Lincoln's Inn Fields, where Bysshe, his mother, and Elizabeth joined us, and a very happy month we spent. Bysshe was full of life and spirits, and very well pleased with his successful devotion to my sister. In the course of that summer, to the best of my recollection, after we had retired into Wiltshire, a continual

correspondence was going on, as I believe, between Bysshe and
my sister Harriet. But she became uneasy at the tone of his letters
on speculative subjects, at first consulting my mother, and subsequently my father also, on the subject. This led at last, though I
cannot exactly tell how, to the dissolution of an engagement between Bysshe and my sister which had previously been permitted
both by his father and mine.

We have here, I think, as unimpassioned a damsel as may be
met in a summer's day. And now let us see the poems.

First, the dedication of *Queen Mab*: bearing in mind that the
poem was begun in 1812, and finished in 1813, and that, to say
nothing of the unsuitability of the offering to her who two years
before had abhorred him as a sceptic and married a clod, she
had never done or said any one thing that would justify her love
being described as that which had warded off from him the
scorn of the world: quite the contrary: as far as in her lay, she
had embittered it to the utmost.

TO HARRIET * * * * *

Whose is the love that, gleaming thro' the world,
Wards off the poisonous arrow of its scorn?
Whose is the warm and partial praise,
Virtue's most sweet reward?

Beneath whose looks did my reviving soul
Riper in truth and virtuous daring grow?
Whose eyes have I gazed fondly on,
And loved mankind the more?

Harriet! on thine:—thou wert my purer mind,
Thou wert the inspiration of my song;
Thine are these early wilding flowers,
Though garlanded by me.

Then press into thy breast this pledge of love,
And know, though time may change and years may roll
Each flowret gathered in my heart
In consecrates to thine.

Next the verses on F. G.:—

> Her voice did quiver as we parted,
> Yet knew I not that heart was broken
> From which it came, and I departed,
> Heeding not the words then spoken.
> Misery—oh, Misery!
> This world is all too wide for thee!

Can anything be more preposterously inappropriate to his parting with Harriet Grove? These verses relate to a far more interesting person and a deeply tragic event; but they belong, as I have said, to the year 1817, a later period than this article embraces.

From Oxford the two friends proceeded to London, where they took a joint lodging, in which, after a time, Shelley was left alone, living uncomfortably on precarious resources. It was here that the second Harriet consoled him for the loss of the first, who, I feel thoroughly convinced, never more troubled his repose.

To the circumstances of Shelley's first marriage I find no evidence but in my own recollection of what he told me respecting it. He often spoke to me of it; and with all allowance for the degree in which his imagination coloured events, I see no improbability in the narration.

Harriet Westbrook, he said, was a schoolfellow of one of his sisters; and when, after his expulsion from Oxford, he was in London, without money, his father having refused him all assistance, this sister had requested her fair schoolfellow to be the medium of conveying to him such small sums as she and her sisters could afford to send, and other little presents which they thought would be acceptable. Under these circumstances the ministry of the young and beautiful girl presented itself like that of a guardian angel, and there was a charm about their intercourse which he readily persuaded himself could not be exhausted in the duration of life. The result was that in August, 1811, they eloped to Scotland, and were married in Edinburgh.* Their journey had absorbed their stock of money. They took a

---

* Not at Gretna Green, as stated by Captain Medwin.

3

lodging, and Shelley immediately told the landlord who they were, what they had come for, and the exhaustion of their resources, and asked him if he would take them in, and advance them money to get married and to carry them on till they could get a remittance. This the man agreed to do, on condition that Shelley would treat him and his friends to a supper in honour of the occasion. It was arranged accordingly; but the man was more obtrusive and officious than Shelley was disposed to tolerate. The marriage was concluded, and in the evening Shelley and his bride were alone together, when the man tapped at their door. Shelley opened it, and the landlord said to him— 'It is customary here at weddings for the guests to come in, in the middle of the night, and wash the bride with whisky.' 'I immediately,' said Shelley, 'caught up my brace of pistols, and pointing them both at him, said to him, "I have had enough of your impertinence; if you give me any more of it I will blow your brains out"; on which he ran or rather tumbled down stairs, and I bolted the doors.'

The custom of washing the bride with whisky is more likely to have been so made known to him than to have been imagined by him.

Leaving Edinburgh, the young couple led for some time a wandering life. At the lakes they were kindly received by the Duke of Norfolk, and by others through his influence. They then went to Ireland, landed at Cork, visited the lakes of Killarney, and stayed some time in Dublin, where Shelley became a warm repealer and emancipator. They then went to the Isle of Man, then to Nant Gwillt* in Radnorshire, then to Lynmouth

---

* Nant Gwillt, the Wild Brook, flows into the Elan (a tributary of the Wye), about five miles above Rhayader. Above the confluence, each stream runs in a rocky channel through a deep narrow valley. In each of these valleys is or was a spacious mansion, named from the respective streams. Cwm Elan House was the seat of Mr Grove, whom Shelley had visited there before his marriage in 1811. Nant Gwillt House, when Shelley lived in it in 1812, was inhabited by a farmer, who let some of the best rooms in lodgings. At a subsequent period I stayed a day in Rhayader, for the sake of seeing this spot. It is a scene of singular beauty.

near Barnstaple,* then came for a short time to London; then went to reside in a furnished house belonging to Mr Madocks at Tanyrallt,† near Tremadoc, in Caernarvonshire. Their residence at this place was made chiefly remarkable by an imaginary attack on his life, which was followed by their immediately leaving Wales.

Mr Hogg inserts several letters relative to this romance of a night: the following extract from one of Harriet Shelley's, dated from Dublin, March 12th, 1813, will give a sufficient idea of it:

Mr Shelley promised you a recital of the horrible events that caused us to leave Wales. I have undertaken the task, as I wish to spare him, in the present nervous state of his health, everything that can recall to his mind the horrors of that night, which I will relate.

On the night of the 26th February we retired to bed between ten and eleven o'clock. We had been in bed about half an hour, when Mr. S—— heard a noise proceeding from one of the parlours. He immediately went down stairs with two pistols which he had loaded that night, expecting to have occasion for them. He went into the billiard-room, when he heard footsteps retreating; he followed into another little room, which was called an office. He there saw a man in the act of quitting the room through a glass window which opened into the shrubbery; the man fired at Mr S——, which he avoided. Bysshe then fired, but it flashed in the pan. The man then knocked Bysshe down, and they struggled on the ground. Bysshe then fired his second pistol, which he thought wounded him in the shoulder, as he uttered a shriek and got up, when he said these words — 'By God, I will be revenged. I will murder your wife, and will ravish your sister! By God, I will be revenged!' He then fled, as we hoped for the night. Our servants were not gone to bed, but were just going when this horrible affair happened. This was about eleven o'clock. We all assembled in the parlour, where we remained for two hours. Mr S—— then advised us to retire, thinking it was impossible he would make a

---

* He had introduced himself by letter to Mr Godwin, and they carried on a correspondence some time before they met. Mr Godwin, after many pressing invitations, went to Lynmouth on an intended visit, but when he arrived the birds had flown.

† *Tan-yr-allt* — Under the precipice.

second attack. We left Bysshe and our manservant—who had only arrived that day, and who knew nothing of the house—to sit up. I had been in bed three hours when I heard a pistol go off. I immediately ran down stairs, when I perceived that Bysshe's flannel gown had been shot through, and the window-curtain. Bysshe had sent Daniel to see what hour it was, when he heard a noise at the window; he went there, and a man thrust his arm through the glass and fired at him. Thank heaven! the ball went through his gown and he remained unhurt. Mr S—— happened to stand sideways; had he stood fronting, the ball must have killed him. Bysshe fired his pistol, but it would not go off; he then aimed a blow at him with an old sword which we found in the house. The assassin attempted to get the sword from him, and just as he was pulling it away Dan rushed into the room, when he made his escape. This was at four in the morning. It had been a most dreadful night; the wind was as loud as thunder, and the rain descended in torrents. Nothing has been heard of him, and we have every reason to believe it was no stranger, as there is a man...who, the next morning, went and told the shopkeepers that it was a tale of Mr Shelley's to impose upon them, that he might leave the country without paying his bills. This they believed, and none of them attempted to do anything towards his discovery. We left Tanyrallt on Sunday.

Mr Hogg subjoins:

Persons acquainted with the localities and with the circumstances, and who had carefully investigated the matter, were unanimous in the opinion that no such attack was ever made.

I may state more particularly the result of the investigation to which Mr Hogg alludes. I was in North Wales in the summer of 1813, and heard the matter much talked of. Persons who had examined the premises on the following morning had found that the grass of the lawn appeared to have been much trampled and rolled on, but there were no footmarks on the wet ground, except between the beaten spot and the window; and the impression of the ball on the wainscot showed that the pistol had been fired towards the window, and not from it. This appeared conclusive as to the whole series of operations having taken place from within. The mental phenomena in which this sort of semi-delusion originated will be better illustrated by one which occurred at a later period, and which, though less tragical in its appearances, was more circumstantial in its development, and more perseveringly adhered to. It will not come within the scope of this article.

I saw Shelley for the first time in 1812, just before he went to Tanyrallt. I saw him again once or twice before I went to North Wales in 1813. On my return he was residing at Bracknell, and invited me to visit him there. This I did, and found him with his wife Harriet, her sister Eliza, and his newly-born daughter Ianthe.

Mr Hogg says:

> This accession to his family did not appear to afford him any gratification, or to create an interest. He never spoke of this child to me, and to this hour I never set eyes on her.

Mr Hogg is mistaken about Shelley's feelings as to his first child. He was extremely fond of it, and would walk up and down a room with it in his arms for a long time together, singing to it a monotonous melody of his own making, which ran on the repetition of a word of his own making. His song was 'Yáhmani, Yáhmani, Yáhmani, Yáhmani'.* It did not please me, but, what was more important, it pleased the child, and lulled it when it was fretful. Shelley was extremely fond of his children. He was pre-eminently an affectionate father. But to this first-born there were accompaniments which did not please him. The child had a wet-nurse whom he did not like, and was much looked after by his wife's sister, whom he intensely disliked. I have often thought that if Harriet had nursed her own child, and if this sister had not lived with them, the link of their married love would not have been so readily broken. But of this hereafter, when we come to speak of the separation.

At Bracknell, Shelley was surrounded by a numerous society,

---

* The tune was the uniform repetition of three notes, not very true in their intervals. The nearest resemblance to it will be found in the second, third, and fourth of a minor key: B C D, for example, on the key of A natural: a crotchet and two quavers.

all in a great measure of his own opinions in relation to religion and politics, and the larger portion of them in relation to vegetable diet. But they wore their rue with a difference. Every one of them adopting some of the articles of the faith of their general church, had each nevertheless some predominant crotchet of his or her own, which left a number of open questions for earnest and not always temperate discussion. I was sometimes irreverent enough to laugh at the fervour with which opinions utterly unconducive to any practical result were battled for as matters of the highest importance to the well-being of mankind; Harriet Shelley was always ready to laugh with me, and we thereby both lost caste with some of the more hot-headed of the party. Mr Hogg was not there during my visit, but he knew the whole of the persons there assembled, and has given some account of them under their initials, which for all public purposes are as well as their names.

The person among them best worth remembering was the gentleman whom Mr Hogg calls J. F. N., of whom he relates some anecdotes.

I will add one or two from my own experience. He was an estimable man and an agreeable companion, and he was not the less amusing that he was the absolute impersonation of a single theory, or rather of two single theories rolled into one. He held that all diseases and all aberrations, moral and physical, had their origin in the use of animal food and of fermented and spirituous liquors; that the universal adoption of a diet of roots, fruits, and distilled* water, would restore the golden age of universal health, purity, and peace; that this most ancient and sublime morality was mystically inculcated in the most ancient Zodiac, which was that of Dendera; that this Zodiac was divided into two hemispheres, the upper hemisphere being the realm of Oromazes or the principle of good, the lower that of Ahrimanes or the principle of evil; that each of these hemispheres was again

---

* He held that water in its natural state was full of noxious impurities, which were only to be got rid of by distillation.

divided into two compartments, and that the four lines of division radiating from the centre were the prototype of the Christian cross. The two compartments of Oromazes were those of Uranus or Brahma the Creator, and of Saturn or Veishnu the Preserver. The two compartments of Ahrimanes were those of Jupiter or Seva the Destroyer, and of Apollo or Krishna the Restorer. The great moral doctrine was thus symbolized in the Zodiacal signs:—In the first compartment, Taurus the Bull, having in the ancient Zodiac a torch in his mouth, was the type of eternal light. Cancer the Crab was the type of celestial matter, sleeping under the all-covering water, on which Brahma floated in a lotus-flower for millions of ages. From the union, typified by Gemini, of light and celestial matter, issued in the second compartment Leo, Primogenial Love, mounted on the back of a Lion, who produced the pure and perfect nature of things in Virgo, and Libra the Balance denoted the coincidence of the ecliptic with the equator, and the equality of man's happy existence. In the third compartment, the first entrance of evil into the system was typified by the change of celestial into terrestrial matter—Cancer into Scorpio. Under this evil influence man became a hunter, Sagittarius the Archer, and pursued the wild animals, typified by Capricorn. Then, with animal food and cookery, came death into the world, and all our woe. But in the fourth compartment, Dhanwantari or Æsculapius, Aquarius the Waterman, arose from the sea, typified by Pisces the Fish, with a jug of pure water and a bunch of fruit, and brought back the period of universal happiness under Aries the Ram, whose benignant ascendancy was the golden fleece of the Argonauts, and the true talisman of Oromazes.

He saw the Zodiac in everything. I was walking with him one day on a common near Bracknell, when we came on a public-house which had the sign of the Horse-shoes. They were four on the sign, and he immediately determined that this number had been handed down from remote antiquity as representative of the compartments of the Zodiac. He stepped into the public-house, and said to the landlord, 'Your sign is the Horse-shoes?'

—'Yes, sir.' 'This sign has always four Horse-shoes?'—'Why mostly, sir.' 'Not always?'—'I think I have seen three.' 'I cannot divide the Zodiac into three. But it is mostly four. Do you know why it is mostly four?'—'Why, sir, I suppose because a horse has four legs.' He bounced out in great indignation, and as soon as I joined him, he said to me, 'Did you ever see such a fool?'

I have also very agreeable reminiscences of Mrs B. and her daughter Cornelia. Of these ladies Shelley says (Hogg, ii. 515):

> I have begun to learn Italian again. Cornelia assists me in this language. Did I not once tell you that I thought her cold and reserved? She is the reverse of this, as she is the reverse of everything bad. She inherits all the divinity of her mother.

Mr Hogg 'could never learn why Shelley called Mrs B. Meimouné.' In fact he called her, not Meimouné, but Maimuna, from Southey's *Thalaba*:

> Her face was as a damsel's face,
> And yet her hair was grey.

She was a young-looking woman for her age, and her hair was as white as snow.

About the end of 1813, Shelley was troubled by one of his most extraordinary delusions. He fancied that a fat old woman who sat opposite to him in a mail coach was afflicted with elephantiasis, that the disease was infectious and incurable, and that he had caught it from her. He was continually on the watch for its symptoms; his legs were to swell to the size of an elephant's, and his skin was to be crumpled over like goose-skin. He would draw the skin of his own hands, arms, and neck very tight, and if he discovered any deviation from smoothness, he would seize the person next to him, and endeavour by a corresponding pressure to see if any corresponding deviation existed. He often startled young ladies in an evening party by this singular process, which was as instantaneous as a flash of lightning.

His friends took various methods of dispelling the delusion. I quoted to him the words of Lucretius:

> Est elephas morbus, qui propter flumina Nili
> Gignitur Aegypto in media, *neque praeterea usquam.*

He said these verses were the greatest comfort he had. When he found that, as the days rolled on, his legs retained their proportion, and his skin its smoothness, the delusion died away.

I have something more to say belonging to this year 1813, but it will come better in connexion with the events of the succeeding year. In the meantime I will mention one or two traits of character in which chronology is unimportant.

It is to be remarked that, with the exception of the clergyman from whom he received his first instructions, the Reverend Mr Edwards, of Horsham, Shelley never came, directly or indirectly, under any authority, public or private, for which he entertained, or had much cause to entertain, any degree of respect. His own father, the Brentford schoolmaster, the head master of Eton, the Master and Fellows of his college at Oxford, the Lord Chancellor Eldon, all successively presented themselves to him in the light of tyrants and oppressors. It was perhaps from the recollection of his early preceptor that he felt a sort of poetical regard for country clergymen, and was always pleased when he fell in with one who had a sympathy with him in classical literature, and was willing to pass *sub silentio* the debateable ground between them. But such an one was of rare occurrence. This recollection may also have influenced his feeling under the following transitory impulse.

He had many schemes of life. Amongst them all, the most singular that ever crossed his mind was that of entering the church. Whether he had ever thought of it before, or whether it only arose on the moment, I cannot say: the latter is most probable; but I well remember the occasion. We were walking in the early summer through a village where there was a good vicarage house, with a nice garden, and the front wall of the vicarage was covered with corchorus in full flower, a plant less common then than it has since become. He stood some time admiring the vicarage wall. The extreme quietness of the scene, the pleasant pathway through the village churchyard, and the brightness of the summer morning, apparently concurred to produce the impression under which he suddenly said to me,—'I feel strongly inclined to enter the church.' 'What,' I said, 'to become a clergyman, with your ideas of the faith?' 'Assent to the supernatural part of it,' he said, 'is merely technical. Of the moral doctrines of Christianity I am a more decided disciple than many of its more ostentatious professors. And consider for a moment how much good a good clergyman may do. In his teaching as a scholar and a moralist; in his example as a gentleman and a man of regular life; in the consolation of his personal intercourse and of his charity among the poor, to whom he may often prove a most beneficent friend when they have no other to comfort them. It is an admirable institution that admits the possibility of diffusing such men over the surface of the land. And am I to deprive myself of the advantages of this admirable institution because there are certain technicalities to which I cannot give my adhesion, but which I need not bring prominently forward? I told him I thought he would find more restraint in the office than would suit his aspirations. He walked on some time thoughtfully, then started another subject, and never returned to that of entering the church.

He was especially fond of the novels of Brown—Charles Brockden Brown, the American, who died at the age of thirty-nine.

The first of these novels was *Wieland*. Wieland's father passed much of his time alone in a summer-house, where he died of spontaneous combustion. This summer-house made a great impression on Shelley, and in looking for a country house he always examined if he could find such a summer-house, or a place to erect one.

The second was *Ormond*. The heroine of this novel, Constantia Dudley, held one of the highest places, if not the very highest place, in Shelley's idealities of female character.

The third was *Edgar Huntley; or, the Sleepwalker*. In this his imagination was strangely captivated by the picture of Clitheroe in his sleep digging a grave under a tree.

The fourth was *Arthur Mervyn*: chiefly remarkable for the powerful description of the yellow fever in Philadelphia and the adjacent country, a subject previously treated in *Ormond*. No descriptions of pestilence surpass these of Brown. The transfer of the hero's affections from a simple peasant-girl to a rich Jewess, displeased Shelley extremely, and he could only account for it on the ground that it was the only way in which Brown could bring his story to an uncomfortable conclusion. The three preceding tales had ended tragically.

These four tales were unquestionably works of great genius, and were remarkable for the way in which natural causes were made to produce the semblance of supernatural effects. The superstitious terror of romance could scarcely be more strongly excited than by the perusal of *Wieland*.

Brown wrote two other novels, *Jane Talbot* and *Philip Stanley*, in which he abandoned this system, and confined himself to the common business of life. They had little comparative success.

Brown's four novels, Schiller's *Robbers*, and Goethe's *Faust*, were, of all the works with which he was familiar, those which took the deepest root in his mind, and had the strongest influence in the formation of his character. He was an assiduous student of the great classical poets, and among these his favourite heroines were Nausicaa and Antigone. I do not remember that he greatly admired any of our old English poets, excepting Shakespeare and Milton. He devotedly admired Wordsworth and Coleridge, and in a minor degree Southey: these had great influence on his style, and Coleridge especially on his imagination; but admiration is one thing and assimilation is another; and nothing so blended itself with the structure of his interior mind as the creations of Brown. Nothing stood so clearly before his thoughts as a perfect combination of the purely ideal and possibly real, as Constantia Dudley.

He was particularly pleased with Wordsworth's Stanzas

written in a pocket copy of Thomson's *Castle of Indolence*. He said the fifth of these stanzas always reminded him of me. I told him the four first stanzas were in many respects applicable to him. He said: 'It was a remarkable instance of Wordsworth's insight into nature, that he should have made intimate friends of two imaginary characters so essentially dissimilar, and yet severally so true to the actual characters of two friends, in a poem written long before they were known to each other, and while they were both boys, and totally unknown to him.'

The delight of Wordsworth's first personage in the gardens of the happy castle, the restless spirit that drove him to wander, the exhaustion with which he returned and abandoned himself to repose, might all in these stanzas have been sketched to the life from Shelley. The end of the fourth stanza is especially apposite:

> Great wonder to our gentle tribe it was
> Whenever from our valley he withdrew;
> For happier soul no living creature has
> Than he had, being here the long day through.
> Some thought he was a lover, and did woo:
> *Some thought far worse of him, and judged him wrong:*
> *But verse was what he had been wedded to;*
> *And his own mind did like a tempest strong*
> *Come to him thus, and drive the weary wight along.*

He often repeated to me, as applicable to himself, a somewhat similar passage from *Childe Harold*:

> On the sea
> The boldest steer but where their ports invite:
> But there are wanderers o'er Eternity,
> Whose bark drives on and on, and anchor'd ne'er shall be.

His vegetable diet entered for something into his restlessness. When he was fixed in a place he adhered to this diet consistently and conscientiously, but it certainly did not agree with him; it made him weak and nervous, and exaggerated the sensitiveness of his imagination. Then arose those thick-coming fancies which almost invariably preceded his change of place. While he was living from inn to inn he was obliged to live, as he said 'on what he could get'; that is to say, like other people. When he got well under this process he gave all the credit to locomotion, and held himself to have thus benefited, not in consequence of his change of regimen, but in spite of it. Once, when I was living in the country, I received a note from him wishing me to call on him in London. I did so, and found him ill in bed. He said, 'You are looking well. I suppose you go on in your old way, living on animal food and fermented liquor?' I answered in the affirmative. 'And here,' he said, 'you see a vegetable feeder overcome by disease.' I said, 'Perhaps the diet is the cause.' This he would by no means allow; but it was not long before he was again posting through some yet unvisited wilds, and recovering his health as usual, by living 'on what he could get'.

He had a prejudice against theatres which I took some pains to overcome. I induced him one evening to accompany me to a representation of the *School for Scandal*. When, after the scenes which exhibited Charles Surface in his jollity, the scene returned, in the fourth act, to Joseph's library, Shelley said to me 'I see the purpose of this comedy. It is to associate virtue with bottles and glasses, and villainy with books.' I had great difficulty to make him stay to the end. He often talked of 'the withering and perverting spirit of comedy'. I do not think he ever went to another. But I remember his absorbed attention to Miss O'Neill's performance of Bianca in *Fazio*, and it is evident to me that she was always in his thoughts when he drew the character of Beatrice in the *Cenci*.

In the season of 1817, I persuaded him to accompany me to the opera. The performance was *Don Giovanni*. Before it commenced he asked me if the opera was comic or tragic. I said it was composite, more comedy than tragedy. After the killing of the Commendatore, he said, 'Do you call this comedy?' By degrees he became absorbed in the music and action. I asked him what he thought of Ambrogetti? He said, 'He seems to be the very wretch he personates.' The opera was followed by a ballet, in which Mdlle Milanie was the principal *danseuse*. He was enchanted with this lady; said he had never imagined such grace of motion; and the impression was permanent, for in a letter he afterwards wrote to me from Milan he said, 'They have no Mdlle Milanie here.'

From this time till he finally left England he was an assiduous frequenter of the Italian Opera. He delighted in the music of Mozart, and especially in the *Nozze di Figaro*, which was performed several times in the early part of 1818.

With the exception of *Fazio*, I do not remember his having been pleased with any performance at an English theatre. Indeed I do not remember his having been present at any but the two above mentioned. I tried in vain to reconcile him to comedy. I repeated to him one day, as an admirable specimen of diction and imagery, Michael Perez's soliloquy in his miserable lodgings, from *Rule a Wife and Have a Wife*. When I came to the passage:

> There's an old woman that's now grown to marble,
> Dried in this brick-kiln: and she sits i' the chimney
> (Which is but three tiles, raised like a house of cards),
> The true proportion of an old smoked Sibyl.
> There is a young thing, too, that Nature meant
> For a maid-servant, but 'tis now a monster:
> She has a husk about her like a chestnut,
> With laziness, and living under the line here:
> And these two make a hollow sound together,
> Like frogs, or winds between two doors that murmur—

he said, 'There is comedy in its perfection. Society grinds down poor wretches into the dust of abject poverty, till they are scarcely recognizable as human beings; and then, instead of being treated as what they really are, subjects of the deepest pity, they are brought forward as grotesque monstrosities to be laughed at.' I said, 'You must admit the fineness of the expression.' 'It is true,' he answered; 'but the finer it is the worse it is, with such a perversion of sentiment.'

I postpone, as I have intimated, till after the appearance of Mr Hogg's third and fourth volumes, the details of the circumstances which preceded Shelley's separation from his first wife, and those of the separation itself.

There never was a case which more strongly illustrated the truth of Payne Knight's observation, that 'the same kind of marriage, which usually ends a comedy, as usually begins a tragedy'.*

---

* No person in his senses was ever led into enterprises of dangerous importance by the romantic desire of imitating the fictions of a drama. If the conduct of any persons is influenced by the examples exhibited in such fictions, it is that of young ladies in the affairs of love and marriage: but I believe that such influence is much more rare than severe moralists are inclined to suppose; since there were plenty of elopements and stolen matches before comedies or plays of any kind were known. If, however, there are any romantic minds which feel this influence, they may draw an awful lesson concerning its consequences from the same source, namely, that the same kind of marriage, which usually ends a comedy, as usually begins a tragedy. (*Principles of Taste,* Book III, c. 2, sec. 17.)

PART II

Y Gwir yn erbyn y Byd.
The Truth against the World.
BARDIC MAXIM.

M R H O G G 's third and fourth volumes not having appeared, and the materials with which Sir Percy and Lady Shelley had supplied him having been resumed by them, and so much of them as it was thought desirable to publish having been edited by Lady Shelley,* with a connecting thread of narrative, I shall assume that I am now in possession of all the external information likely to be available towards the completion of my memoir; and I shall proceed to complete it accordingly, subject to the contingent addition of a postscript, if any subsequent publication should render it necessary.

Lady Shelley says in her preface:

> We saw the book (Mr Hogg's) for the first time when it was given to the world. It was impossible to imagine beforehand that from such materials a book could have been produced which has astonished and shocked those who have the greatest right to form an opinion on the character of Shelley; and it was with the most painful feelings of dismay that we perused what we could only look upon as a fantastic caricature, going forth to the public with my apparent sanction,—for it was dedicated to myself.
>
> Our feelings of duty to the memory of Shelley left us no other alternative than to withdraw the materials which we had originally

---

* *Shelley Memorials.* From Authentic Sources. Edited by Lady Shelley. London: Smith and Elder. 1859.

entrusted to his early friend, and which we could not but consider had been strangely misused; and to take upon ourselves the task of laying them before the public, connected only by as slight a thread of narrative as would suffice to make them intelligible to the reader.

I am very sorry, in the outset of this notice, to be under the necessity of dissenting from Lady Shelley respecting the facts of the separation of Shelley and Harriet.

Captain Medwin represented this separation to have taken place by mutual consent. Mr Leigh Hunt and Mr Middleton adopted this statement; and in every notice I have seen of it in print it has been received as an established truth.

Lady Shelley says:

> Towards the close of 1813 estrangements, which for some time had been slowly growing between Mr and Mrs Shelley, came to a crisis. Separation ensued, and Mrs Shelley returned to her father's house. Here she gave birth to her second child — a son, who died in 1826.
>
> The occurrences of this painful epoch in Shelley's life, and of the causes which led to them, I am spared from relating. In Mary Shelley's own words — 'This is not the time to relate the truth; and I should reject any colouring of the truth. No account of these events has ever been given at all approaching reality in their details, either as regards himself or others; nor shall I further allude to them than to remark that the errors of action committed by a man as noble and generous as Shelley, may, as far as he only is concerned be fearlessly avowed by those who loved him, in the firm conviction that, were they judged impartially, his character would stand in fairer and brighter light than that of any contemporary.'
>
> Of those remaining who were intimate with Shelley at this time, each has given us a different version of this sad event, coloured by his own views or personal feelings. Evidently Shelley confided to none of these friends. We, who bear his name, and are of his family, have in our possession papers written by his own hand, which in after years may make the story of his life complete; and which few now living, except Shelley's own children, have ever perused.
>
> One mistake, which has gone forth to the world, we feel ourselves called upon positively to contradict.
>
> Harriet's death has sometimes been ascribed to Shelley. This is

entirely false. There was no immediate connexion whatever between her tragic end and any conduct on the part of her husband.
It is true, however, that it was a permanent source of the deepest
sorrow to him; for never during all his after-life did the dark shade
depart which had fallen on his gentle and sensitive nature from the
self-sought grave of the companion of his early youth.

This passage ends the sixth chapter. The seventh begins thus:

To the family of Godwin, Shelley had, from the period of his
self-introduction at Keswick, been an object of interest; and the
acquaintanceship which had sprung up between them during the
poet's occasional visits to London had grown into a cordial friendship. It was in the society and sympathy of the Godwins that
Shelley sought and found some relief in his present sorrow. He
was still extremely young. His anguish, his isolation, his difference
from other men, his gifts of genius and eloquent enthusiasm, made
a deep impression on Godwin's daughter Mary, now a girl of sixteen, who had been accustomed to hear Shelley spoken of as something rare and strange. To her, as they met one eventful day in
St Pancras' churchyard, by her mother's grave, Bysshe, in burning
words, poured forth the tale of his wild past—how he had suffered,
how he had been misled; and how, if supported by her love, he
hoped in future years to enrol his name with the wise and good
who had done battle for their fellow-men, and been true through
all adverse storms to the cause of humanity.

Unhesitatingly she placed her hand in his, and linked her
fortune with his own; and most truthfully, as the remaining portion of these *Memorials* will prove, was the pledge of both redeemed.

I ascribe it to inexperience of authorship, that the sequence of
words does not, in these passages, coincide with the sequence of
facts: for in the order of words, the present sorrow would appear
to be the death of Harriet. This however occurred two years and
a half after the separation, and the union of his fate with Mary
Godwin was simultaneous with it. Respecting this separation,
whatever degree of confidence Shelley may have placed in his
several friends, there are some facts which speak for themselves
and admit of no misunderstanding.

The Scotch marriage had taken place in August, 1811. In a
letter which he wrote to a female friend sixteen months later
(Dec. 10, 1812), he had said:

How is Harriet a fine lady? You indirectly accuse her in your letter of this offence — to me the most unpardonable of all. The ease and simplicity of her habits, the unassuming plainness of her address, the uncalculated connexion of her thought and speech, have ever formed in my eyes her greatest charms: and none of these are compatible with fashionable life, or the attempted assumption of its vulgar and noisy *éclat*. You have a prejudice to contend with in making me a convert to this last opinion of yours, which, so long as I have a living and daily witness to its futility before me, I fear will be insurmountable. (*Memorials*, p. 44.)

Thus there had been no estrangement to the end of 1812. My own memory sufficiently attests that there was none in 1813.

From Bracknell, in the autumn of 1813, Shelley went to the Cumberland lakes; then to Edinburgh. In Edinburgh he became acquainted with a young Brazilian named Baptista, who had gone there to study medicine by his father's desire, and not from any vocation to the science, which he cordially abominated, as being all hypothesis, without the fraction of a basis of certainty to rest on. They corresponded after Shelley left Edinburgh, and subsequently renewed their intimacy in London. He was a frank, warm-hearted, very gentlemanly young man. He was a great enthusiast, and sympathized earnestly in all Shelley's views, even to the adoption of vegetable diet. He made some progress in a translation of *Queen Mab* into Portuguese. He showed me a sonnet, which he intended to prefix to his translation. It began:

Sublime Shelley, cantor di verdade!

and ended:

Surja *Queen Mab* a restaurar o mundo.

I have forgotten the intermediate lines. But he died early, of a disease of the lungs. The climate did not suit him, and he exposed himself to it incautiously.

Shelley returned to London shortly before Christmas, then took a furnished house for two or three months at Windsor, visiting London occasionally. In March, 1814, he married

Harriet a second time, according to the following certificate:

MARRIAGES IN MARCH, 1814.

164. Percy Bysshe Shelley and Harriet Shelley (formerly Harriet Westbrook, Spinster, a Minor), both of this Parish, were remarried in this Church by Licence (the parties having been already married to each other according to the Rites and Ceremonies of the Church of Scotland), in order to obviate all doubts that have arisen, or shall or may arise, touching or concerning the validity of the aforesaid Marriage (by and with the consent of John Westbrook, the natural and lawful father of the said Minor), this Twenty-fourth day of March, in the Year 1814.

By me,

EDWARD WILLIAMS, Curate.

This Marriage was solemnized between us { PERCY BYSSHE SHELLEY, HARRIET SHELLEY, formerly Harriet Westbrook.

In the presence of { JOHN WESTBROOK, JOHN STANLEY.

The above is a true extract from the Register Book of Marriages belonging to the Parish of Saint George, Hanover-square; extracted thence this eleventh day of April, 1859. — By me,

H. WEIGHTMAN, Curate.

It is, therefore, not correct to say that 'estrangements which had been slowly growing came to a crisis towards the close of 1813'. The date of the above certificate is conclusive on the point. The second marriage could not have taken place under such circumstances. Divorce would have been better for both parties, and the dissolution of the first marriage could have been easily obtained in Scotland.

There was no estrangement, no shadow of a thought of separation, till Shelley became acquainted, not long after the second marriage, with the lady who was subsequently his second wife.

The separation did not take place by mutual consent. I cannot think that Shelley ever so represented it. He never did so to me: and the account which Harriet herself gave me of the entire proceeding was decidedly contradictory of any such supposition.

He might well have said, after first seeing Mary Wollstone-craft Godwin, '*Ut vidi! ut perii!*' Nothing that I ever read in tale or history could present a more striking image of a sudden, violent, irresistible, uncontrollable passion, than that under which I found him labouring when, at his request, I went up from the country to call on him in London. Between his old feelings towards Harriet, *from whom he was not then separated*, and his new passion for Mary, he showed in his looks, in his gestures, in his speech, the state of a mind 'suffering, like a little kingdom, the nature of an insurrection'. His eyes were blood-shot, his hair and dress disordered. He caught up a bottle of laudanum, and said: 'I never part from this.'* He added: 'I am always repeating to myself your lines from Sophocles:

> Man's happiest lot is not to be:
>   And when we tread life's thorny steep,
> Most blest are they, who earliest free
>   Descend to death's eternal sleep.'

---

* In a letter to Mr Trelawny, dated June 18th, 1822, Shelley says: 'You of course enter into society at Leghorn. Should you meet with any scientific person capable of preparing the *Prussic Acid, or Essential Oil of Bitter Almonds*, I should regard it as a great kindness if you could procure me a small quantity. It requires the greatest caution in prepa-ration, and ought to be highly concentrated. I would give any price for this medicine. You remember we talked of it the other night, and we both expressed a wish to possess it. My wish was serious, and sprung from the desire of avoiding needless suffering. I need not tell you I have no intention of suicide at present; but I confess it would be a comfort to me to hold in my possession that golden key to the chamber of perpetual rest. The *Prussic Acid* is used in medicine in infinitely minute doses; but that preparation is weak, and has not the concen-tration necessary to medicine all ills infallibly. A single drop, even less, is a dose, and it acts by paralysis.' (*Trelawny*, pp. 100, 101.)

I believe that up to this time he had never travelled without pistols for defence, nor without laudanum as a refuge from intolerable pain. His physical suffering was often very severe; and this last letter must have been written under the anticipation that it might become incur-able, and unendurable to a degree from which he wished to be perma-nently provided with the means of escape.

Again, he said more calmly: 'Every one who knows me must know that the partner of my life should be one who can feel poetry and understand philosophy. Harriet is a noble animal, but she can do neither.' I said, 'It always appeared to me that you were very fond of Harriet.' Without affirming or denying this, he answered: 'But you did not know how I hated her sister.'

The term 'noble animal' he applied to his wife, in conversation with another friend now living, intimating that the nobleness which he thus ascribed to her would induce her to acquiesce in the inevitable transfer of his affections to their new shrine. She did not so acquiesce, and he cut the Gordian knot of the difficulty by leaving England with Miss Godwin on the 28th of July, 1814.

Shortly after this I received a letter from Harriet, wishing to see me. I called on her at her father's house in Chapel-street, Grosvenor-square. She then gave me her own account of the transaction, which, as I have said, decidedly contradicted the supposition of anything like separation by mutual consent.

She at the same time gave me a description, by no means flattering, of Shelley's new love, whom I had not then seen. I said, 'If you have described her correctly, what could he see in her?' 'Nothing,' she said, 'but that her name was Mary, and not only Mary, but Mary Wollstonecraft.'

The lady had nevertheless great personal and intellectual attractions, though it is not to be wondered at that Harriet could not see them.

I feel it due to the memory of Harriet to state my most decided conviction that her conduct as a wife was as pure, as true, as absolutely faultless, as that of any who for such conduct are held most in honour.

Mr Hogg says: 'Shelley told me his friend Robert Southey once said to him, "A man ought to be able to live with any woman. You see that I can, and so ought you. It comes to pretty much the same thing, I apprehend. There is no great choice or difference." ' (*Hogg*: vol. i, p. 423). *Any woman*, I suspect, must have been said with some qualification. But such a one as either of them had first chosen, Southey saw no reason to change.

Shelley gave me some account of an interview he had had with Southey. It was after his return from his first visit to Switzerland, in the autumn of 1814. I forget whether it was in town or country; but it was in Southey's study, in which was suspended a portrait of Mary Wollstonecraft. Whether Southey had been in love with this lady, is more than I know. That he had devotedly admired her is clear from his *Epistle to Amos Cottle*, prefixed to the latter's *Icelandic Poetry* (1797); in which, after describing the scenery of Norway, he says:

> Scenes like these
> Have almost lived before me, when I gazed
> Upon their fair resemblance traced by him,
> Who sung the banished man of Ardebeil;
> Or to the eye of Fancy held by her,
> Who among women left no equal mind
> When from this world she passed; and I could weep
> To think that she is to the grave gone down!

where a note names Mary Wollstonecraft, the allusion being to her *Letters from Norway*.

Shelley had previously known Southey, and wished to renew or continue friendly relations; but Southey was repulsive. He pointed to the picture, and expressed his bitter regret that the daughter of that angelic woman should have been so misled. It was most probably on this occasion that he made the remark cited by Mr Hogg: his admiration of Mary Wollstonecraft may have given force to the observation: and as he had known Harriet, he might have thought that, in his view of the matter, she was all that a husband could wish for.

Few are now living who remember Harriet Shelley. I remember her well, and will describe her to the best of my recollection. She had a good figure, light, active, and graceful. Her features were regular and well proportioned. Her hair was light brown, and dressed with taste and simplicity. In her dress she was truly *simplex munditiis*. Her complexion was beautifully transparent; the tint of the blush rose shining through the lily. The tone of her voice was pleasant; her speech the essence of frankness and cordiality; her spirits always cheerful; her laugh spontaneous, hearty, and joyous. She was well educated. She read agreeably and intelligently. She wrote only letters, but she wrote them well. Her manners were good; and her whole aspect and demeanour such manifest emanations of pure and truthful nature, that to be once in her company was to know her thoroughly. She was fond of her husband, and accommodated herself in every way to his tastes. If they mixed in society, she adorned it; if they lived in retirement, she was satisfied; if they travelled, she enjoyed the change of scene.

That Shelley's second wife was intellectually better suited to him than his first, no one who knew them both will deny; and that a man, who lived so totally out of the ordinary world and in a world of ideas, needed such an ever-present sympathy more than the general run of men, must also be admitted; but Southey, who did not want an intellectual wife, and was contented with his own, may well have thought that Shelley had equal reason to seek no change.

After leaving England, in 1814, the newly-affianced lovers took a tour on the Continent. He wrote to me several letters from Switzerland, which were subsequently published, together with a *Six Weeks' Tour*, written in the form of a journal by the lady with whom his fate was thenceforward indissolubly bound. I was introduced to her on their return.

The rest of 1814 they passed chiefly in London. Perhaps this winter in London was the most solitary period of Shelley's life. I often passed an evening with him at his lodgings, and I do not recollect ever meeting any one there, excepting Mr Hogg. Some of his few friends of the preceding year had certainly at that time fallen off from him. At the same time he was short of money, and was trying to raise some on his expectations, from

'Jews and their fellow-Christians', as Lord Byron says. One day, as we were walking together on the banks of the Surrey Canal, and discoursing of Wordsworth, and quoting some of his verses, Shelley suddenly said to me: 'Do you think Wordsworth could have written such poetry, if he had ever had dealings with money-lenders?' His own example, however, proved that the association had not injured his poetical faculties.

The canal in question was a favourite walk with us. The Croydon Canal branched off from it, and passed very soon into wooded scenery. The Croydon Canal is extinct, and has given place to the, I hope, more useful, but certainly less picturesque, railway. Whether the Surrey exists, I do not know. He had a passion for sailing paper-boats, which he indulged on this canal, and on the Serpentine river. The best spot he had ever found for it was a large pool of transparent water, on a heath above Bracknell, with determined borders free from weeds, which admitted of launching the miniature craft on the windward, and running round to receive it on the leeward, side. On the Serpentine, he would sometimes launch a boat constructed with more than usual care, and freighted with halfpence. He delighted to do this in the presence of boys, who would run round to meet it, and when it landed in safety, and the boys scrambled for their prize, he had difficulty in restraining himself from shouting as loudly as they did. The river was not suitable to this amusement, nor even Virginia Water, on which he sometimes practised it; but the lake was too large to allow of meeting the landing. I sympathized with him in this taste: I had it before I knew him: I am not sure that I did not originate it with him; for which I should scarcely receive the thanks of my friend, Mr Hogg, who never took any pleasure in it, and cordially abominated it, when, as frequently happened, on a cold winter day, in a walk from Bishopgate over Bagshot Heath, we came on a pool of water, which Shelley would not part from till he had rigged out a flotilla from any unfortunate letters he happened to have in his pocket. Whatever may be thought of this amusement for grown gentlemen, it was at least innocent amusement, and not mixed up with any 'sorrow of the meanest thing that feels'.*

In the summer of 1815, Shelley took a furnished house at Bishopgate, the eastern entrance of Windsor Park, where he resided till the summer of 1816. At this time he had, by the sacrifice of a portion of his expectations, purchased an annuity of £1000 a year from his father, who had previously allowed him £200.

I was then living at Marlow, and frequently walked over to pass a few days with him. At the end of August, 1815, we made an excursion on the Thames to Lechlade, in Gloucestershire, and as much higher as there was water to float our skiff. It was a dry season, and we did not get much beyond Inglesham Weir, which was not then, as now, an immovable structure, but the wreck of a movable weir, which had been subservient to the navigation, when the river had been, as it had long ceased to be, navigable to Cricklade. A solitary sluice was hanging by a chain, swinging in the wind and creaking dismally. Our voyage terminated at a spot where the cattle stood entirely across the stream, with the water scarcely covering their hoofs. We started from, and returned to, Old Windsor, and our excursion occupied about ten days. This was, I think, the origin of Shelley's taste for boating, which he retained to the end of his life. On our way up, at Oxford, he was so much out of order that he feared being obliged to return. He had been living chiefly on tea and bread and butter, drinking occasionally a sort of spurious lemonade, made of some powder in a box, which, as he was reading at the time the *Tale of a Tub*, he called *the powder of pimperlimpimp*. He consulted a doctor, who may have done him some good, but it was not apparent. I told him, 'If he would allow me to prescribe for him, I would set him to rights.' He asked, 'What

---

*This lesson, shepherd, let us two divide,
Taught both by what she† shows and what conceals,
Never to blend our pleasure or our pride
With sorrow of the meanest thing that feels.
              WORDSWORTH, *Hartleap Well.*
† Nature.

would be your prescription?' I said, 'Three mutton chops, well peppered.' He said, 'Do you really think so?' I said, 'I am sure of it.' He took the prescription; the success was obvious and immediate. He lived in my way for the rest of our expedition, rowed vigorously, was cheerful, merry, overflowing with animal spirits, and had certainly one week of thorough enjoyment of life. We passed two nights in a comfortable inn at Lechlade, and his lines, *A Summer Evening on the Thames at Lechlade*, were written then and there. Mr Shelley (the second, who always bore his name), who was with us, made a diary of the little trip, which I suppose is lost.

The whole of the winter 1815-16 was passed quietly at Bishopgate. Mr Hogg often walked down from London; and I, as before, walked over from Marlow. This winter was, as Mr Hogg expressed it, a mere Atticism. Our studies were exclusively Greek. To the best of my recollection, we were, throughout the whole period, his only visitors. One or two persons called on him; but they were not to his mind, and were not encouraged to reappear. The only exception was a physician whom he had called in; the Quaker, Dr Pope, of Staines. This worthy old gentleman came more than once, not as a doctor, but a friend. He liked to discuss theology with Shelley. Shelley at first avoided the discussion, saying his opinions would not be to the Doctor's taste; but the Doctor answered, 'I like to hear thee talk, friend Shelley; I see thee art very deep.'

At this time Shelley wrote his *Alastor*. He was at a loss for a title, and I proposed that which he adopted: *Alastor; or, the Spirit of Solitude*. The Greek word Ἀλάστωρ is an evil genius, κακοδαίμων, though the sense of the two words is somewhat different, as in the Φανεὶς Ἀλάστπρ ἢ κακὸς δαίμων ποθέν, of Aeschylus. The poem treated the spirit of solitude as a spirit of evil. I mention the true meaning of the word because many have supposed *Alastor* to be the name of the hero of the poem.

He published this, with some minor poems, in the course of the winter.

In the early summer of 1816, the spirit of restlessness again came over him, and resulted in a second visit to the Continent. The change of scene was preceded, as more than once before, by a mysterious communication from a person seen only by himself, warning him of immediate personal perils to be incurred by him if he did not instantly depart.

I was alone at Bishopgate, with him and Mrs Shelley, when the visitation alluded to occurred. About the middle of the day, intending to take a walk, I went into the hall for my hat. His was there, and mine was not. I could not imagine what had become of it; but as I could not walk without it, I returned to the library. After some time had elapsed, Mrs Shelley came in, and gave me an account which she had just received from himself, of the visitor and his communication. I expressed some scepticism on the subject, on which she left me, and Shelley came in, with my hat in his hand. He said, 'Mary tells me, you do not believe that I have had a visit from Williams.' I said, 'I told her there were some improbabilities in the narration.' He said, 'You know Williams of Tremadoc?' I said, 'I do.' He said, 'It was he who was here to-day. He came to tell me of a plot laid by my father and uncle, to entrap me and lock me up. He was in great haste, and could not stop a minute, and I walked with him to Egham.' I said, 'What hat did you wear?' He said, 'This, to be sure.' I said, 'I wish you would put it on.' He put it on, and it went over his face. I said, 'You could not have walked to Egham in that hat.' He said, 'I snatched it up hastily, and perhaps I kept it in my hand. I certainly walked with Williams to Egham, and he told me what I have said. You are very sceptical.' I said, 'If you are certain of what you say, my scepticism cannot affect your certainty.' He said, 'It is very hard on a man who has devoted his life to the pursuit of truth, who has made great sacrifices and incurred great sufferings for it, to be treated as a visionary. If I do not know that I saw Williams, how do I know that I see you?' I said, 'An idea may have the force of a sensation; but the oftener a sensation is repeated, the greater is the probability of its origin in reality. You saw me yesterday, and will see me to-morrow.' He said, 'I can see Williams to-morrow if I please. He told me he was stopping at the Turk's Head Coffee-house, in the Strand, and should be there two days. I want to convince you that I am not under a delusion. Will you walk with me to London to-morrow, to see him?' I said, 'I would most willingly do so.' The next morning after an early breakfast we set off on our walk to London. We had got halfway down Egham-hill, when he suddenly turned round, and said to me, 'I do not think we shall find Williams at the Turk's Head.' I said, 'Neither do I.' He said, 'You say that, because you do not think he has been there; but he mentioned a contingency under which he might leave town yesterday, and he has probably done so.' I said, 'At any rate, we should know that he has been there.' He said, 'I will take other means of convincing you. I will write to him. Suppose we take a walk through the forest.' We turned about on our new direction, and were out all day. Some days passed, and I heard no more of the matter. One morning he said to me, 'I have some news of Williams; a letter and an enclosure.' I said, 'I shall be glad to see the letter.' He said, 'I cannot show you the letter; I will show you the enclosure. It is a diamond necklace. I think you know me well enough to be sure I would not throw away my own money on such a thing, and that if I have it, it must have been sent me by somebody else. It has been sent me by Williams.' 'For what purpose?' I asked. He said, 'To prove his identity and his sincerity.' 'Surely,' I said, 'your showing me a diamond necklace will prove nothing but that you have one to show.' 'Then,' he said, 'I will not show it you. If you will not believe me, I must submit to your incredulity.' There the matter ended. I never heard another word of Williams, nor of any other mysterious visitor. I had on one or two previous occasions argued with him against similar semi-delusions, and I believe if they had always been received with similar scepticism, they would not have been often repeated; but they were encouraged by the ready credulity with which they were received by many, who ought to have known better. I call them semi-delusions, because, for the most part, they had their basis in his firm belief that his father and uncle had designs on his liberty. On this basis, his imagination built a fabric of romance, and when he presented it as substantive fact, and it was found to contain more or less of inconsistency, he felt his self-esteem interested in maintaining it by accumulated circumstances, which severally vanished under the touch of investigation, like Williams's location at the Turk's Head Coffee-house.

I must add, that in the expression of these differences, there was not a shadow of anger. They were discussed with freedom and calmness; with the good temper and good feeling which never forsook him in conversations with his friends. There was an evident anxiety for acquiescence, but a quiet and gentle toleration of dissent. A personal discussion, however interesting to himself, was carried on with the same calmness as if it related to the most abstract question in metaphysics.

Indeed, one of the great charms of intercourse with him was the perfect good humour and openness to conviction with which he responded to opinions opposed to his own. I have known eminent men, who were no doubt very instructive as lecturers to people who like being lectured; which I never did; but with whom conversation was impossible. To oppose their dogmas, even to question them, was to throw their temper off its balance. When once this infirmity showed itself in any of my friends, I was always careful not to provoke a second ebullition. I submitted to the preachment, and was glad when it was over.

The result was a second trip to Switzerland. During his absence he wrote me several letters, some of which were subsequently published by Mrs Shelley; others are still in my possession. Copies of two of these were obtained by Mr Middleton, who has printed a portion of them. Mrs Shelley was at that time in the habit of copying Shelley's letters, and these were among some papers accidentally left at Marlow, where they fell into unscrupulous hands. Mr Middleton must have been aware that he had no right to print them without my consent. I might have stopped his publication by an injunction, but I did not think it worth while, more especially as the book, though abounding with errors adopted from Captain Medwin and others, is written with good feeling towards the memory of Shelley.

During his stay in Switzerland he became acquainted with Lord Byron. They made together an excursion round the lake of Geneva, of which he sent me the detail in a diary. This diary was published by Mrs Shelley, but without introducing the name of Lord Byron, who is throughout called 'my companion'. The diary was first published during Lord Byron's life; but why his name was concealed I do not know. Though the changes are not many, yet the association of the two names gives it great additional interest.

At the end of August, 1816, they returned to England, and Shelley passed the first fortnight of September with me at Marlow. July and August, 1816, had been months of perpetual rain. The first fortnight of September was a period of unbroken sunshine. The neighbourhood of Marlow abounds with beautiful walks; the river scenery is also fine. We took every day a long excursion, either on foot or on the water. He took a house there, partly, perhaps principally, for the sake of being near me. While it was being fitted and furnished, he resided at Bath.

In December, 1816, Harriet drowned herself in the Serpentine river, not, as Captain Medwin says, in a pond at the bottom of her father's garden at Bath. Her father had not then left his house in Chapel-street, and to that house his daughter's body was carried.

On the 30th of December, 1816, Shelley married his second wife; and early in the ensuing year they took possession of their house at Marlow. It was a house with many large rooms and extensive gardens. He took it on a lease for twenty-one years, furnished it handsomely, fitted up a library in a room large enough for a ball-room, and settled himself down, as he supposed, for life. This was an agreeable year to all of us. Mr Hogg was a frequent visitor. We had a good deal of rowing and sailing, and we took long walks in all directions. He had other visitors from time to time. Amongst them were Mr Godwin and Mr and Mrs Leigh Hunt. He led a much more social life than he had done at Bishopgate; but he held no intercourse with his immediate neighbours. He said to me more than once, 'I am not wretch enough to tolerate an acquaintance.'

In the summer of 1817 he wrote the *Revolt of Islam*, chiefly on a seat on a high prominence in Bisham Wood, where he passed whole mornings with a blank book and a pencil. This work, when completed, was printed under the title of *Laon and Cythna*. In this poem he had carried the expression of his opinions, moral, political, and theological, beyond the bounds of discretion. The terror which, in those days of persecution of the press, the perusal of the book inspired in Mr Ollier, the publisher, induced him to solicit the alteration of many passages which he had marked. Shelley was for some time inflexible; but Mr Ollier's refusal to publish the poem as it was, backed by the advice of all his friends, induced him to submit to the required changes. Many leaves were cancelled, and it was finally published as *The Revolt of Islam*. Of *Laon and Cythna* only three copies had gone forth. One of these had found its way to the *Quarterly Review*, and the opportunity was readily seized of pouring out on it one of the most malignant effusions of the *odium theologicum* that ever appeared even in those days, and in that periodical.

During his residence at Marlow we often walked to London, frequently in company with Mr Hogg. It was our usual way of going there, when not pressed by time. We went by a very pleasant route over fields, lanes, woods, and heaths to Uxbridge, and by the main road from Uxbridge to London. The total distance was thirty-two miles to Tyburn turnpike. We usually stayed two nights, and walked back on the third day. I never saw Shelley tired with these walks. Delicate and fragile as he appeared, he had great muscular strength. We took many walks in all directions from Marlow, and saw everything worth seeing within a radius of sixteen miles. This comprehended, among other notable places, Windsor Castle and Forest, Virginia

4

Water, and the spots which were consecrated by the memories of Cromwell, Hampden, and Milton, in the Chiltern district of Buckinghamshire. We had also many pleasant excursions, rowing and sailing on the river, between Henley and Maidenhead.

Shelley, it has been seen, had two children by his first wife. These children he claimed after Harriet's death, but her family refused to give them up. They resisted the claim in Chancery, and the decree of Lord Eldon was given against him.

The grounds of Lord Eldon's decision have been misrepresented. The petition had adduced *Queen Mab*, and other instances of Shelley's opinions on religion, as one of the elements of the charges against him; but the judgment ignores this element, and rests entirely on moral conduct. It was distinctly laid down that the principles which Shelley had professed in regard to some of the most important relations of life, had been carried by him into practice; and that the practical development of those principles, not the principles themselves, had determined the judgment of the Court.

Lord Eldon intimated that his judgment was not final; but nothing would have been gained by an appeal to the House of Peers. Liberal law lords were then unknown; neither could Shelley have hoped to enlist public opinion in his favour. A Scotch marriage, contracted so early in life, might not have been esteemed a very binding tie: but the separation which so closely followed on a marriage in the Church of England, contracted two years and a half later, presented itself as the breach of a much more solemn and deliberate obligation.

It is not surprising that so many persons at the time should have supposed that the judgment had been founded, at least partly, on religious grounds. Shelley himself told me, that Lord Eldon had expressly stated that such grounds were excluded, and the judgment itself showed it. But few read the judgment. It did not appear in the newspapers, and all report of the proceedings was interdicted. Mr Leigh Hunt accompanied Shelley to the Court of Chancery. Lord Eldon was extremely courteous; but he said blandly, and at the same time determinedly, that a report of the proceedings would be punished as a contempt of Court. The only explanation I have ever been able to give to myself of his motive for this prohibition was, that he was willing to leave the large body of fanatics among his political supporters under delusion as to the grounds of his judgment; and that it was more for his political interest to be stigmatized by Liberals as an inquisitor, than to incur in any degree the imputation of theological liberality from his own persecuting party.

Since writing the above passages I have seen, in the *Morning Post* of November 22nd, the report of a meeting of the Juridical Society, under the presidency of the present Lord Chancellor, in which a learned brother read a paper, proposing to revive the system of persecution against 'blasphemous libel'; and in the course of his lecture he said: 'The Court of Chancery, on the doctrine *Parens patriae*, deprived the parent of the guardianship of his children when his principles were in antagonism to religion, as in the case of the poet Shelley.' The Attorney-General observed on this: 'With respect to the interference of the Court of Chancery in the case of Shelley's children, there was a great deal of misunderstanding. It was not because their father was an unbeliever in Christianity, but because he violated and refused to acknowledge the ordinary usages of morality.' The last words are rather vague and twaddling, and I suppose are not the *ipsissima verba* of the Attorney-General. The essence and quintessence of Lord Eldon's judgment was this: 'Mr Shelley long ago published and maintained the doctrine that marriage is a contract binding only during mutual pleasure. He has carried out that doctrine in his own practice; he has done nothing to show that he does not still maintain it; and I consider such practice injurious to the best interests of society.' I am not apologizing for Lord Eldon, nor vindicating his judgment. I am merely explaining it, simply under the wish that those who talk about it should know what it really was.

Some of Shelley's friends have spoken and written of Harriet as if to vindicate him it were necessary to disparage her. They might, I think, be content to rest the explanation of his conduct on the ground on which he rested it himself—that he had found in another the intellectual qualities which constituted his ideality of the partner of his life. But Harriet's untimely fate occasioned him deep agony of mind, which he felt the more because for a long time he kept the feeling to himself. I became acquainted with it in a somewhat singular manner.

I was walking with him one evening in Bisham Wood, and we had been talking, in the usual way, of our ordinary subjects, when he suddenly fell into a gloomy reverie. I tried to rouse him out of it, and made some remarks which I thought might make him laugh at his own abstraction. Suddenly he said to me, still with the same gloomy expression: 'There is one thing to which I have decidedly made up my mind. I will take a great glass of ale every night.' I said, laughingly, 'A very good resolution, as the result of a melancholy musing.' 'Yes,' he said; 'but you do not know why I take it. I shall do it to deaden my feelings: for I see that those who drink ale have none.' The next day he said to me: 'You must have thought me very unreasonable yesterday evening?' I said, 'I did, certainly.' 'Then,' he said, 'I will tell you what I would not tell any one else. I was thinking of Harriet.' I told him, 'I had no idea of such a thing: it was so long since he had named her. I had thought he was under the influence of some baseless morbid feeling; but if ever I should see him again in such a state of mind, I would not attempt to disturb it.'

There was not much comedy in Shelley's life; but his anti-pathy to 'acquaintance' led to incidents of some drollery. Amongst the persons who called on him at Bishopgate, was one whom he tried hard to get rid of, but who forced himself on him in every possible manner. He saw him at a distance one day, as he was walking down Egham Hill, and instantly jumped through a hedge, ran across a field, and laid himself down in a dry ditch. Some men and women, who were haymaking in the field, ran up to see what was the matter, when he said to them, 'Go away, go away: don't you see it's a bailiff?' On which they left him, and he escaped discovery.

After he had settled himself at Marlow, he was in want of a music-master to attend a lady staying in his house, and I inquired for one at Maidenhead. Having found one, I requested that he would call on Mr Shelley. One morning Shelley rushed into my house in great trepidation, saying: 'Barricade the doors; give orders that you are not at home. Here is ―― in the town.' He passed the whole day with me, and we sat in expectation that the knocker or the bell would announce the unwelcome visitor; but the evening fell on the unfulfilled fear. He then ventured home. It turned out that the name of the music-master very nearly resembled in sound the name of the obnoxious gentleman; and when Shelley's man opened the library door and said, 'Mr ――, sir,' Shelley, who caught the name as that of his *Monsieur Tonson*, exclaimed, 'I would just as soon see the devil!', sprang up from his chair, jumped out of the window, ran across the lawn, climbed over the garden-fence, and came round to me by a back path: when we entrenched ourselves for a day's siege. We often laughed afterwards at the thought of what must have been his man's astonishment at seeing his master, on the announcement of the musician, disappear so instantaneously through the window, with the exclamation, 'I would just as soon see the devil!', and in what way he could explain to the musician that his master was so suddenly 'not at home'.

Shelley, when he did laugh, laughed heartily, the more so as what he considered the perversions of comedy excited not his laughter but his indignation, although such disgusting outrages on taste and feeling as the burlesques by which the stage is now disgraced had not then been perpetrated. The ludicrous, when it neither offended good feeling, nor perverted moral judgment, necessarily presented itself to him with greater force.

Though his published writings are all serious, yet his letters are not without occasional touches of humour. In one which he wrote to me from Italy, he gave an account of a new acquaintance who had a prodigious nose. 'His nose is something quite Slawken-nergian. It weighs on the imagination to look at it. It is that sort of nose that transforms all the g's its wearer utters into k's. It is a nose once seen never to be forgotten, and which requires the utmost stretch of Christian charity to forgive. I, you know, have a little turn-up nose, H—— has a large hook one; but add them together, square them, cube them, you would have but a faint notion of the nose to which I refer.'

I may observe incidentally, that his account of his own nose corroborates the opinion I have previously expressed of the inadequate likeness of the published portraits of him, in which the nose has no turn-up. It had, in fact, very little; just as much as may be seen in the portrait to which I have referred, in the Florentine Gallery.

The principal employment of the female population in Marlow was lace-making, miserably remunerated. He went continually amongst this unfortunate population, and to the extent of his ability relieved the most pressing cases of distress. He had a list of pensioners, to whom he made a weekly allowance.

Early in 1818 the spirit of restlessness again came over him. He left Marlow, and, after a short stay in London, left England in March of that year, never to return.

I saw him for the last time, on Tuesday the 10th of March. The evening was a remarkable one, as being that of the first performance of an opera of Rossini in England, and of the first appearance here of Malibran's father, Garcia. He performed Count Almaviva in the *Barbiere di Siviglia*. Fodor was Rosina; Naldi, Figaro; Ambrogetti, Bartolo; and Angrisani, Basilio. I supped with Shelley and his travelling companions after the opera. They departed early the next morning.

Thus two very dissimilar events form one epoch in my memory. In looking back to that long-past time, I call to mind how many friends, Shelley himself included, I saw around me in the old Italian Theatre, who have now all disappeared from the scene. I hope I am not unduly given to be *laudator temporis acti*, yet I cannot but think that the whole arrangement of the opera in England has changed for the worse. Two acts of opera, a divertissement, and a ballet, seem very ill replaced by four or five acts of opera, with little or no dancing. These, to me, verify the old saying, that 'Too much of one thing is good for nothing'; and the quiet and decorous audiences, of whom Shelley used to say, 'It is delightful to see human beings so civilized', are not agreeably succeeded by the vociferous assemblies, calling and recalling performers to the footlights, and showering down bouquets to the accompaniment of their noisy approbation.

At the time of his going abroad, he had two children by his second wife—William and Clara; and it has been said that the fear of having these taken from him by a decree of the Chancellor had some influence on his determination to leave England; but there was no ground for such a fear. No one could be interested in taking them from him; no reason could be alleged for taking them from their mother; the Chancellor would not have entertained the question, unless a provision had been secured for the children; and who was to do this? Restlessness and embarrassment were the causes of his determination; and according to the Newtonian doctrine, it is needless to look for more causes than are necessary to explain the phenomena.

These children both died in Italy: Clara, the youngest, in 1818, William, in the following year. The last event he communicated to me in a few lines, dated Rome, June 8th, 1819:

> Yesterday, after an illness of only a few days, my little William died. There was no hope from the moment of the attack. You will be kind enough to tell all my friends, so that I need not write to them. It is a great exertion to me to write this, and it seems to me as if, hunted by calamity as I have been, that I should never recover any cheerfulness again.

A little later in the same month he wrote to me again from Livorno:

> Our melancholy journey finishes at this town; but we retrace our steps to Florence, where, as I imagine, we shall remain some months. O that I could return to England! How heavy a weight when misfortune is added to exile; and solitude, as if the measure were not full, heaped high on both. O that I could return to England! I hear you say, 'Desire never fails to generate capacity.' Ah! but that ever-present Malthus, necessity, has convinced desire, that even though it generated capacity its offspring must starve.

Again from Livorno; August, 1819 (they had changed their design of going to Florence):

> I most devoutly wish that I were living near London. I don't think that I shall settle so far off as Richmond, and to inhabit any intermediate spot on the Thames, would be to expose myself to the river damps. Not to mention that it is not much to my taste. My inclinations point to Hampstead; but I don't know whether I should not make up my mind to something more completely sub-urban. What are mountains, trees, heaths, or even the glorious and ever-beautiful sky, with such sunsets as I have seen at Hamp-stead, to friends? Social enjoyment in some form or other is the Alpha and Omega of existence. All that I see in Italy, and from my tower window I now see the magnificent peaks of the Apen-nine, half enclosing the plain, is nothing — it dwindles to smoke in the mind, when I think of some familiar forms of scenery, little perhaps in themselves, over which old remembrances have thrown a delightful colour. How we prize what we despised when present! So the ghosts of our dead associations rise and haunt us, in revenge for our having let them starve and abandoned them to perish.

This seems to contrast strangely with a passage in Mrs Shelley's journal, written after her return to England:

> Mine own Shelley! What a horror you had of returning to this miserable country! To be here without you is to be doubly exiled; to be away from Italy is to lose you twice. (*Shelley Memorials*, p. 224.)

It is probable, however, that as Mrs Shelley was fond of Italy, he did not wish to disturb her enjoyment of it, by letting her see fully the deep-seated wish to return to his own country, which lay at the bottom of all his feelings.

It is probable also that, after the birth of his last child, he became more reconciled to residing abroad.

In the same year, the parents received the best consolation which nature could bestow on them, in the birth of another son, the present Sir Percy, who was born at Florence, on the 12th of November, 1819.

Shelley's life in Italy is best traced by his letters. He delighted in the grand aspects of nature; mountains, torrents, forests, and the sea; and in the ruins, which still reflected the greatness of antiquity. He described these scenes with extraordinary power of language, in his letters as well as in his poetry; but in the latter he peopled them with phantoms of virtue and beauty, such as never existed on earth. One of his most striking works in this kind is the *Prometheus Unbound*. He only once descended into the arena of reality, and that was in the tragedy of the *Cenci*.* This is unquestionably a work of great dramatic power, but it is as unquestionably not a work for the modern English stage. It would have been a great work in the days of Massinger. He sent it to me to introduce it to Covent Garden Theatre. I did so; but the result was as I expected. It could not be received; though great admiration was expressed of the author's powers, and great hopes of his success with a less repulsive subject. But he could not clip his wings to the littleness of the acting drama; and though he adhered to his purpose of writing for the stage, and chose Charles I for his subject, he did not make much progress in the task. If his life had been prolonged, I still think he would have accomplished something worthy of the best days of theatrical literature. If the gorgeous scenery of his poetry could have been peopled from actual life, if the deep thoughts and strong feelings which he was so capable of expressing, had been accommodated to characters such as have been and may be, however exceptional in the greatness of passion, he would have added his own name to those of the masters of the art. He studied it with unwearied devotion in its

---

* Horace Smith's estimate of these two works appears to me just: 'I got from Ollier last week a copy of the *Prometheus Unbound*, which is certainly a most original, grand, and occasionally sublime work, evincing in my opinion a higher order of talent than any of your previous productions; and yet, contrary to your own estimation. I must say I prefer the *Cenci*, because it contains a deep and sustained human interest, of which we feel a want in the other. Prometheus himself certainly touches us nearly; but we see very little of him after his liberation; and, though I have no doubt it will be more admired than anything you have written, I question whether it will be so much read as the *Cenci*.' (*Shelley Memorials*, p. 145.)

higher forms; the Greek tragedians, Shakespeare, and Calderon. Of Calderon, he says, in a letter to me from Leghorn, September 21st, 1819:

> C. C. is now with us on his way to Vienna. He has spent a year or more in Spain, where he has learnt Spanish; and I make him read Spanish all day long. It is a most powerful and expressive language, and I have already learnt sufficient to read with great ease their poet Calderon. I have read about twelve of his plays. Some of them certainly deserve to be ranked among the grandest and most perfect productions of the human mind. He excels all modern dramatists, with the exception of Shakespeare, whom he resembles, however, in the depth of thought and subtlety of imagination of his writings, and in the one rare power of inter-weaving delicate and powerful comic traits with the most tragic situations, without diminishing their interest. I rank him far above Beaumont and Fletcher.

In a letter to Mr Gisborne dated November, 1820, he says: 'I am bathing myself in the light and odour of the flowery and starry *Autos*. I have read them all more than once.' These were Calderon's religious dramas, being of the same class as those which were called *Mysteries* in France and England, but of a far higher order of poetry than the latter ever attained.

The first time Mr Trelawny saw him, he had a volume of Calderon in his hand. He was translating some passages of the *Magico Prodigioso*.

> I arrived late, and hastened to the Tre Palazzi, on the Lung' Arno, where the Shelleys and Williamses lived on different flats under the same roof, as is the custom on the Continent. The Williamses received me in their earnest, cordial manner; we had a great deal to communicate to each other, and were in loud and animated conversation, when I was rather put out by observing in the passage near the open door, opposite to where I sat, a pair of glittering eyes steadily fixed on mine; it was too dark to make out whom they belonged to. With the acuteness of a woman, Mrs Williams's eyes followed the direction of mine, and going to the doorway, she laughingly said: 'Come in, Shelley; it's only our friend Tre just arrived.'
>
> Swiftly gliding in, blushing like a girl, a tall, thin stripling held out both his hands; and although I could hardly believe, as I

looked at his flushed, feminine, and artless face, that it could be the poet, I returned his warm pressure. After the ordinary greetings and courtesies he sat down and listened. I was silent from astonishment: was it possible this wild-looking, beardless boy, could be the veritable monster at war with all the world?—excommunicated by the Fathers of the Church, deprived of his civil rights by the fiat of a grim Lord Chancellor, discarded by every member of his family, and denounced by the rival sages of our literature as a founder of a Satanic school? I would not believe it; it must be a hoax. He was habited like a boy, in a black jacket and trousers, which he seemed to have outgrown, or his tailor, as is the custom, had most shamefully stinted him in his 'sizings'. Mrs Williams saw my embarrassment, and to relieve me asked Shelley what book he had in his hand? His face brightened, and he answered briskly:

'Calderon's *Magico Prodigioso*; I am translating some passages in it.'

'Oh, read it to us!'

Shoved off from the shore of commonplace incidents that could not interest him, and fairly launched on a theme that did, he instantly became oblivious of everything but the book in his hand. The masterly manner in which he analysed the genius of the author, his lucid interpretations of the story, and the ease with which he translated into our language the most subtle and imaginative passages of the Spanish poet, were marvellous, as was his command of the two languages. After this touch of his quality, I no longer doubted his identity. A dead silence ensued; looking up, I asked: 'Where is he?'

Mrs Williams said, 'Who? Shelley? Oh, he comes and goes like a spirit, no one knows when or where.' (*Trelawny*, pp. 19–22.)

From this time Mr Trelawny was a frequent visitor to the Shelleys, and, as will be seen, a true and indefatigable friend.

In the year 1818, Shelley renewed his acquaintance with Lord Byron, and continued in friendly intercourse with him till the time of his death. Till that time his life, from the birth of his son Percy, was passed chiefly in or near Pisa, or on the seashore between Genoa and Leghorn. It was unmarked by any remarkable events, except one or two, one of which appears to me to have been a mere disturbance of imagination. This was a story of his having been knocked down at the post office in Florence, by a man in a military cloak, who had suddenly walked up to him, saying, 'Are you the damned atheist Shelley?' This man was not seen by any one else, nor ever afterwards seen or heard of; though a man answering the description had on the same day left Florence for Genoa, and was followed up without success.

I cannot help classing this incident with the Tan-yr-allt assassination, and other semi-delusions, of which I have already spoken.

Captain Medwin thinks this 'cowardly attack' was prompted by some article in the *Quarterly Review*. The Quarterly Reviewers of that day had many sins to answer for in the way of persecution of genius, whenever it appeared in opposition to their political and theological intolerance; but they were, I am satisfied, as innocent of this 'attack' on Shelley, as they were of the death of Keats. Keats was consumptive, and fore-doomed by nature to early death. His was not the spirit 'to let itself be snuffed out by an article'.*

With the cessation of his wanderings, his beautiful descriptive letters ceased also. The fear of losing their only surviving son predominated over the love of travelling by which both parents were characterized. The last of this kind which was addressed to me was dated Rome, March 23rd, 1819. This was amongst the letters published by Mrs Shelley. It is preceded by two from Naples—December 22nd, 1818, and January 26th, 1819. There was a third, which is alluded to in the beginning of his letter from Rome: 'I wrote to you the day before our departure from Naples.' When I gave Mrs Shelley the other letters, I sought in vain for this. I found it, only a few months since, in some other papers, among which it had gone astray.

His serenity was temporarily disturbed by a calumny, which Lord Byron communicated to him. There is no clue to what it was; and I do not understand why it was spoken of at all. A mystery is a riddle, and the charity of the world will always give such a riddle the worst possible solution.

---

* *Don Juan*, c. xi. st. 29.

An affray in the streets of Pisa was a more serious and perilous reality. Shelley was riding outside the gates of Pisa with Lord Byron, Mr Trelawny, and some other Englishmen, when a dragoon dashed through their party in an insolent manner. Lord Byron called him to account. A scuffle ensued, in which the dragoon knocked Shelley off his horse, wounded Captain Hay in the hand, and was dangerously wounded himself by one of Lord Byron's servants. The dragoon recovered; Lord Byron left Pisa; and so ended an affair which might have had very disastrous results.

Under present circumstances the following passage in a letter which he wrote to me from Pisa, dated March, 1820, will be read with interest:

> I have a motto on a ring in Italian: '*Il buon tempo verra.*' There is a tide both in public and in private affairs which awaits both men and nations.
>
> I have no news from Italy. We live here under a nominal tyranny, administered according to the philosophic laws of Leopold, and the mild opinions which are the fashion here. Tuscany is unlike all the other Italian States in this respect.

Shelley's last residence was a villa on the Bay of Spezzia. Of this villa Mr Trelawny has given a view.

Amongst the new friends whom he had made to himself in Italy were Captain and Mrs Williams. To these, both himself and Mrs Shelley were extremely attached. Captain Williams was fond of boating, and furnished a model for a small sailing vessel, which he persisted in adopting against the protest of the Genoese builder and of their friend Captain Roberts, who superintended her construction. She was called the *Don Juan*. It took two tons of iron ballast to bring her down to her bearings, and even then she was very crank in a breeze. Mr Trelawny dispatched her from Genoa under the charge of two steady seamen and a boy named Charles Vivian. Shelley retained the boy and sent back the two sailors. They told Mr Trelawny that she was a ticklish boat to manage, but had sailed and worked well, and that they had cautioned the gentlemen accordingly.

It is clear from Mr Trelawny's account of a trip he had with them, that the only good sailor on board was the boy. They contrived to jam the mainsheet and to put the tiller starboard instead of port. 'If there had been a squall,' he said, 'we should have had to swim for it.'

'Not I,' said Shelley; 'I should have gone down with the rest of the pigs at the bottom of the boat,' meaning the iron pig-ballast.

In the mean time, at the instance of Shelley, Lord Byron had concurred in inviting Mr Leigh Hunt and his family to Italy. They were to co-operate in a new quarterly journal, to which it was expected that the name of Byron would ensure an immediate and extensive circulation. This was the unfortunate *Liberal*, a title furnished by Lord Byron, of which four numbers were subsequently published. It proved a signal failure, for which there were many causes; but I do not think that any name or names could have buoyed it up against the dead weight of its title alone. A literary periodical should have a neutral name, and leave its character to be developed in its progress. A journal might be pre-eminently, on one side or the other, either aristocratical or democratical in its tone; but to call it the *Aristocrat* or the *Democrat* would be fatal to it.

Leigh Hunt arrived in Italy with his family on the 14th of June, 1822, in time to see his friend once and no more.

Shelley was at that time writing a poem called the *Triumph of Life*. The composition of this poem, the perpetual presence of the sea, and other causes (among which I do not concur with Lady Shelley in placing the solitude of his seaside residence, for his life there was less solitary than it had almost ever been),

contributed to plunge the mind of Shelley into a state of morbid excitement, the result of which was a tendency to see visions. One night loud cries were heard issuing from the saloon. The Williamses rushed out of their room in alarm; Mrs Shelley also endeavoured to reach the spot, but fainted at the door. Entering the saloon, the Williamses found Shelley staring horribly into the air, and evidently in a trance. They waked him, and he related that a figure wrapped in a mantle came to his bedside and beckoned him. He must then have risen in his sleep, for he followed the imaginary figure into the saloon, when it lifted the hood of its mantle, ejaculated 'Siete sodisfatto?'* and vanished. The dream is said to have been suggested by an incident occurring in a drama attributed to Calderon.

Another vision appeared to Shelley on the evening of May 6th, when he and Williams were walking together on the terrace. The story is thus recorded by the latter in his diary:

> Fine. Some heavy drops of rain fell without a cloud being visible. After tea, while walking with Shelley on the terrace, and observing the effect of moonshine on the waters, he complained of being unusually nervous, and, stopping short, he grasped me violently by the arm, and stared steadfastly on the white surf that broke upon the beach under our feet. Observing him sensibly affected, I demanded of him if he was in pain; but he only answered by saying 'There it is again! there!' He recovered after some time, and declared that he saw, as plainly as he then saw me, a naked child (Allegra, who had recently died) rise from the sea, and clasp its hands as if in joy, smiling at him. This was a trance that it required some reasoning and philosophy entirely to wake him from, so forcibly had the vision operated on his mind. Our conversation, which had been at first rather melancholy, led to this, and my confirming his sensations by confessing that I had felt the same, gave greater activity to his ever-wandering and lively imagination. (*Shelley Memorials*, pp. 191–3.)

On the afternoon of the 8th of July, 1822, after an absence of some days from home, Shelley and Williams set sail from Leghorn for their home on the Gulf of Spezzia. Trelawny watched them from Lord Byron's vessel, the *Bolivar*. The day was hot and calm. Trelawny said to his Genoese mate, 'They will soon have the land breeze.' 'Maybe,' said the mate, 'they will soon have too much breeze. That gaff-topsail is foolish, in a boat with no deck and no sailor on board. Look at those black lines, and the dirty rags hanging under them out of the sky. Look at the

---

* Are you satisfied?

smoke on the water. The devil is brewing mischief.' Shelley's
boat disappeared in a fog.

> Although the sun was obscured by mists, it was oppressively
> sultry. There was not a breath of air in the harbour. The heaviness
> of the atmosphere, and an unwonted stillness benumbed my
> senses. I went down into the cabin and sank into a slumber. I was
> roused up by a noise over-head and went on deck. The men were
> getting up a chain cable to let go another anchor. There was a
> general stir amongst the shipping; shifting berths, getting down
> yards and masts, veering out cables, hauling in of hawsers, letting
> go anchors, hailing from the ships and quays, boats scudding
> rapidly to and fro. It was almost dark, although only half-past six
> o'clock. The sea was of the colour, and looked as solid and smooth
> as a sheet of lead, and covered with an oily scum. Gusts of wind
> swept over without ruffling it, and big drops of rain fell on its sur-
> face, rebounding, as if they could not penetrate it. There was a
> commotion in the air, made up of many threatening sounds, coming
> upon us from the sea. Fishing-craft and coasting-vessels under
> bare poles rushed by us in shoals, running foul of the ships in the
> harbour. As yet the din and hubbub was that made by men, but
> their shrill pipings were suddenly silenced by the crashing voice
> of a thunder-squall that burst right over our heads. For some
> time no other sounds were to be heard than the thunder, wind
> and rain. When the fury of the storm, which did not last for more
> than twenty minutes, had abated, and the horizon was in some
> degree cleared, I looked to seaward anxiously, in the hope of
> descrying Shelley's boat amongst the many small craft scattered
> about. I watched every speck that loomed on the horizon, thinking
> that they would have borne up on their return to the port, as all
> the other boats that had gone out in the same direction had done.
> (*Trelawny*, pp. 116–18.)

Mrs Shelley and Mrs Williams passed some days in dreadful
suspense. Mrs Shelley, unable to endure it longer, proceeded to
Pisa, and rushing into Lord Byron's room with a face of marble,
asked passionately, 'Where is my husband?' Lord Byron afterwards said, he had never seen anything in dramatic tragedy to
equal the terror of Mrs Shelley's appearance on that day.

At length the worst was known. The bodies of the two friends
and the boy were washed on shore. That of the boy was buried
in the sand. That of Captain Williams was burned on the 15th

of August. The ashes were collected and sent to England for interment. The next day the same ceremony was performed for Shelley; and his remains were collected to be interred, as they subsequently were, in the Protestant cemetery at Rome. Lord Byron and Mr Leigh Hunt were present on both occasions. Mr Trelawny conducted all the proceedings, as he had conducted all the previous search. Herein, and in the whole of his subsequent conduct towards Mrs Shelley, he proved himself, as I have already observed, a true and indefatigable friend. In a letter which she wrote to me, dated Genoa, Sept. 29th, 1822, she said:

> Trelawny is the only quite disinterested friend I have here; the only one who clings to the memory of my loved ones as I do myself; but he, alas! is not [as] one of them, though he is really kind and good.

The boat was subsequently recovered; the state in which everything was found in her, showed that she had not capsized. Captain Roberts first thought that she had been swamped by a heavy sea; but on closer examination, finding many of the timbers on the starboard quarter broken, he thought it certain that she must have been run down by a felucca in the squall.

I think the first conjecture the most probable. Her masts were gone, and her bowsprit broken. Mr Trelawny had previously dispatched two large feluccas with ground-tackling to drag for her. This was done for five or six days. They succeeded in finding her, but failed in getting her up. The task was accomplished by Captain Roberts. The specified damage to such a fragile craft was more likely to have been done by the dredging apparatus, than by collision with a felucca.

So perished Percy Bysshe Shelley, in the flower of his age, and not perhaps even yet in the full flower of his genius; a genius unsurpassed in the description and imagination of scenes of beauty and grandeur; in the expression of impassioned love of ideal beauty; in the illustration of deep feeling by congenial imagery; and in the infinite variety of harmonious versification.

What was, in my opinion, deficient in his poetry was, as I have
already said, the want of reality in the characters with which he
peopled his splendid scenes, and to which he addressed or im-
parted the utterance of his impassioned feelings. He was advancing, I think, to the attainment of this reality. It would have
given to his poetry the only element of truth which it wanted;
though at the same time, the more clear development of what
men were would have lowered his estimate of what they might
be, and dimmed his enthusiastic prospect of the future destiny
of the world. I can conceive him, if he had lived to the present
time, passing his days like Volney, looking on the world from
his windows without taking part in its turmoils; and perhaps
like the same, or some other great apostle of liberty (for I cannot
at this moment verify the quotation), desiring that nothing
should be inscribed on his tomb, but his name, the dates of his
birth and death, and the single word,

'DÉSILLUSIONNÉ.'

SUPPLEMENTARY NOTICE

In *Macmillan's Magazine* for June, 1860, there is an article entitled '*Shelley in Pall-Mall*; by Richard Garnett,' which contains the following passage:

> Much has been written about Shelley during the last three or four years, and the store of materials for his biography has been augmented by many particulars, some authentic and valuable, others trivial or mythical, or founded on mistakes or misrepresentations. It does not strictly fall within the scope of this paper to notice any of these, but some of the latter class are calculated to modify so injuriously what has hitherto been the prevalent estimate of Shelley's character, and, while entirely unfounded, are yet open to correction from the better knowledge of so few, that it would be inexcusable to omit an opportunity of comment which only chance has presented, and which may not speedily recur. It will be readily perceived that the allusion is to the statements respecting Shelley's separation from his first wife, published by Mr T. L. Peacock, in *Fraser's Magazine* for January last. According to these, the transaction was not preceded by long-continued unhappiness, neither was it an amicable agreement effected in virtue of a mutual understanding. The time cannot be distant when these assertions must be refuted by the publication of documents hitherto withheld, and Shelley's family have doubted whether it be worth while to anticipate it. Pending their decision, I may be allowed to state most explicitly that the evidence to which they would in such a case appeal, and to the nature of which I feel fully competent to speak, most decidedly contradicts the allegations of Mr Peacock.

A few facts in the order of time will show, I will not say the extreme improbability, but the absolute impossibility, of Shelley's family being in possession of any such documents as are here alleged to exist.

83

In August, 1811, Shelley married Harriet Westbrook in Scotland.

On the 24th of March, 1814, he married her a second time in the Church of England, according to the marriage certificate printed in my article of January, 1860. This second marriage could scarcely have formed an incident in a series of 'long-continued unhappiness'.

In the beginning of April, 1814, Shelley and Harriet were together on a visit to Mrs B., at Bracknell. This lady and her family were of the few who constituted Shelley's most intimate friends. On the 18th of April, she wrote to Mr Hogg: 'Shelley is again a widower. His beauteous half went to town on Thursday with Miss Westbrook, who is gone to live, I believe, at Southampton.'*

Up to this time, therefore, at least, Shelley and Harriet were together; and Mrs B.'s letter shows that she had no idea of estrangement between them, still less of permanent separation.

I said in my article of January, 1860: 'There was no estrangement, no shadow of a thought of separation, till Shelley became acquainted, not long after the second marriage, with the lady who was subsequently his second wife.'

When Shelley first saw this lady, she had just returned from a visit to some friends in Scotland; and when Mr Hogg first saw her, she wore 'a frock of tartan, an unusual dress in London at that time'.† She could not have been long returned.

Mr Hogg saw Mary Godwin for the first time on the first day of Lord Cochrane's trial. This was the 8th of June, 1814. He went with Shelley to Mr Godwin's. 'We entered a room on the first floor....William Godwin was not at home....The door was partially and softly opened. A thrilling voice called "Shelley!" A thrilling voice answered "Mary!" And he darted out of the room like an arrow from the bow of the far-shooting king.'†

Shelley's acquaintance with Miss Godwin must, therefore,

---

* Hogg's *Life of Shelley*, vol. ii, p. 533.
† Hogg, vol. ii, pp. 537–8.

have begun between the 18th of April and the 8th of June; much nearer, I apprehend, to the latter than the former, but I cannot verify the precise date.

On the 7th of July, 1814, Harriet wrote to a mutual friend, still living, a letter in which 'she expressed a confident belief that he must know where Shelley was, and entreating his assistance to induce him to return home'. She was not even then aware that Shelley had finally left her.

On the 28th of the same month, Shelley and Miss Godwin left England for Switzerland.

The interval between the Scotch and English marriages was two years and seven months. The interval between the second marriage and the departure for Switzerland, was four months and four days. In the estimate of probabilities, the space for voluntary separation is reduced by Mrs B.'s letter of April 18, to three months and thirteen days; and by Harriet's letter of July 7, to twenty-one days. If, therefore, Shelley's family have any document which demonstrates Harriet's consent to the separation, it must prove the consent to have been given on one of these twenty-one days. I know, by my subsequent conversation with Harriet, of which the substance was given in my article of January, 1860, that she was not a consenting party; but as I have only my own evidence to that conversation, Mr Garnett may choose not to believe me. Still, on other evidence than mine, there remain no more than three weeks within which, if at all, the 'amicable agreement' must have been concluded.

But again, if Shelley's family had any conclusive evidence on the subject, they must have had some clear idea of the date of the separation, and of the circumstances preceding it. That they had not, is manifest from Lady Shelley's statement, that 'towards the close of 1813, estrangements, which for some time had been slowly growing between Mr and Mrs Shelley, came to a crisis: separation ensued, and she returned to her father's house.'* Lady Shelley could not have written thus if she had

---

* *Shelley Memorials*, pp. 64–5.

known the date of the second marriage, or had even adverted to the letter of the 18th of April, 1814, which had been published by Mr Hogg long before the production of her own volume.

————

I wrote the preceding note immediately after the appearance of Mr Garnett's article; but I postponed its publication, in the hope of obtaining copies of the letters which were laid before Lord Eldon in 1817. These were nine letters from Shelley to Harriet, and one from Shelley to Miss Westbrook after Harriet's death. These letters were not filed; but they are thus alluded to in Miss Westbrook's affidavit, dated 10th January, 1817, of which I have procured a copy from the Record Office:

> Elizabeth Westbrook, of Chapel-street, Grosvenor-square, in the parish of Saint George, Hanover-square, in the county of Middlesex, spinster, maketh oath and saith, that she knows and is well acquainted with the handwriting of Percy Bysshe Shelley, Esquire, one of the defendants in this cause, having frequently seen him write; and this deponent saith that she hath looked upon certain paper writings now produced, and shown to her at the time of swearing this her affidavit, and marked respectively 1, 2, 3, 4, 5, 6, 7, 8, 9; and this deponent saith that the female mentioned or referred to in the said letters, marked respectively 2, 4, 6, 9, under the name or designation of 'Mary', and in the said other letters by the character or description of the person with whom the said defendant had connected or associated himself, is Mary Godwin, in the pleadings of this cause named, whom the said defendant, Percy Bysshe Shelley, in the life-time of his said wife, and in or about the middle of the year 1814, took to cohabit with him, and hath ever since continued to cohabit, and still doth cohabit with; and this deponent saith that she hath looked upon a certain other paper writing, produced and shown to this deponent now at the time of swearing this her affidavit, and marked 10; and this deponent saith that the same paper writing is of the handwriting of the said defendant, Percy Bysshe Shelley, and was addressed by him to this deponent, since the decease of her said sister, the late wife of the said Percy Bysshe Shelley. And this deponent saith that the person referred to in the said last

mentioned letter as '*the Lady whose union with the said defendant this deponent might excusably regard as the cause of her Sister's Ruin*', is also the said Mary Godwin.

The rest of the affidavit relates to *Queen Mab*.

The words marked in italics could not possibly have been written by Shelley, if his connexion with Miss Godwin had not been formed till after a separation from Harriet by mutual consent.

In a second affidavit, dated 13th January, 1817, Miss Westbrook stated in substance the circumstances of the marriage, and that two children were the issue of it: that after the birth of the first child, Eliza Ianthe, and while her sister was pregnant with the second, Charles Bysshe, Percy Bysshe Shelley deserted his said wife, and cohabited with Mary Godwin; and thereupon Harriet returned to the house of her father, with her eldest child, and soon afterwards the youngest child was born there; that the children had always remained under the protection of Harriet's father, and that Harriet herself had resided under the same protection until a short time previous to her death in December, 1816. It must be obvious that this statement could not have been made if the letters previously referred to had not borne it out; if, in short, they had not demonstrated, first, that the separation was not by mutual consent; and secondly, that it followed, not preceded, Shelley's first acquaintance with Mary Godwin. The rest of the affidavit related to the provision which Mr Westbrook had made for the children.

Harriet suffered enough in her life to deserve that her memory should be respected. I have always said to all whom it might concern, that I would defend her, to the best of my ability, against all misrepresentations. Such are not necessary to Shelley's vindication. That is best permitted to rest, as I have already observed, on the grounds on which it was placed by himself.*

---

* *Fraser's Magazine*, January, 1860, p. 102.

The *Quarterly Review* for October, 1861, has an article on Shelley's life and character, written in a tone of great fairness and impartiality, with an evident painstaking to weigh evidence and ascertain truth. There are two passages in the article, on which I wish to offer remarks, with reference solely to matters of fact.

> Shelley's hallucinations, though not to be confounded with what is usually called insanity, are certainly not compatible with perfect soundness of mind. They were the result of an excessive sensibility, which, only a little more severely strained, would have overturned reason altogether. It has been said that the horror of his wife's death produced some such effect, and that for a time at least he was actually insane. Lady Shelley says nothing about this, and we have no explicit statement of the fact by any authoritative biographer. But it is not in itself improbable (p. 323).

It was not so, however. He had at that time taken his house at Marlow, where I was then living. He was residing in Bath, and I was looking after the fitting-up of the house and the laying out of the grounds. I had almost daily letters from him or Mary. He was the first to tell me of Harriet's death, asking whether I thought it would become him to interpose any delay before marrying Mary. I gave him my opinion that, as they were living together, the sooner they legalized their connexion the better. He acted on this opinion, and shortly after his marriage he came to me at Marlow. We went together to see the progress of his house and grounds. I recollect a little scene which took place on this occasion. There was on the lawn a very fine old wide-spreading holly. The gardener had cut it up into a bare pole, selling the lop for Christmas decorations. As soon as Shelley saw it, he asked the gardener, 'What had possessed him to ruin that beautiful tree?' The gardener said, he thought he had improved its appearance. Shelley said: 'It is impossible that you can be such a fool.' The culprit stood twiddling his thumbs along the seams of his trousers, receiving a fulminating denunciation, which ended in his peremptory dismissal. A better man was engaged, with several assistants, to make an extensive plantation of shrubs. Shelley stayed with me two or three days. I never saw him more calm and self-possessed. Nothing disturbed his serenity but the unfortunate holly. Subsequently, the feeling for Harriet's death grew into a deep and abiding sorrow: but it was not in the beginning that it was felt most strongly.

> It is not merely as a work of art that the *Revolt of Islam* must be considered. It had made its first appearance under the title of *Laon and Cythna*, but *Laon and Cythna* was still more outspoken as to certain matters than the *Revolt of Islam*, and was almost immediately withdrawn from circulation, to appear with alterations under its present name. There is something not quite worthy of Shelley in this transaction. On the one hand, merely prudential reasons, mere dread of public indignation, ought not to have induced him to conceal opinions which for the interest of humanity he thought it his duty to promulgate. But those who knew most of Shelley will be least inclined to attribute to him such a motive as this. On the other hand, if good feeling induced him to abstain from printing what he knew must be painful to the great majority of his countrymen, the second version should have been suppressed as well as the first. (pp. 314–15.)

Shelley was not influenced by either of the motives supposed. Mr Ollier positively refused to publish the poem as it was, and Shelley had no hope of another publisher. He for a long time refused to alter a line: but his friends finally prevailed on him to submit. Still he could not, or would not, sit down by himself to alter it, and the whole of the alterations were actually made in successive sittings of what I may call a literary committee. He contested the proposed alterations step by step: in the end, sometimes adopting, more frequently modifying, never originating, and always insisting that his poem was spoiled.

AN ESSAY
ON FASHIONABLE
LITERATURE

AN ESSAY ON
FASHIONABLE LITERATURE

I. The fashionable metropolitan winter, which begins in spring and ends in autumn, is the season of happy re-union to those ornamental varieties of the human species who live to be amused for the benefit of social order. It is the period of the general muster, the levy *en masse* of gentlemen in stays and ladies in short petticoats against their arch enemy Time. It is the season of operas and exhibitions, of routs and concerts, of dinners at midnight and suppers at sunrise. But these are the arms with which they assail the enemy in battalion: there are others with which in moments of morning solitude they are compelled to encounter him single-handed: and one of these weapons is the reading of light and easy books which command attention without the labour of application, and amuse the idleness of fancy without disturbing the sleep of understanding.

II. This species of literature, which aims only to amuse and must be very careful not to instruct, had never so many purveyors as at present: for there never was any state of society in which there were so many idle persons as there are at present in England, and it happens that these idle persons are for the most part so circumstanced that they can do nothing if they would, and in the next place that they are united in the links of a common interest which, being based in delusion, makes them even more averse than the well-dressed vulgar always are from the free exercise of reason and the bold investigation of truth.

III. That the faculty of amusing should be the only passport of a literary work into the hands of general readers is not very

surprising, more especially when we consider that the English is
the most thinking people in the universe: but that the faculty of
amusing should be as transient as the gloss of a new coat does
seem at first view a little singular: for though all fashionable
people read (gentlemen who have been at college excepted), yet
as the soul of fashion is novelty, the books and the dress of the
season go out of date together; and to be amused this year by
that which amused others twelve months ago would be to plead
guilty to the heinous charge of having lived out of the world.

IV. The stream of new books, therefore, floats over the parlour window, the boudoir sofa, and the drawing-room table to
furnish a ready answer to the question of Mr. Donothing as to
what Mrs Dolittle and her daughters are reading, and having
served this purpose, and that of putting the monster Time to a
temporary death, flows peacefully on towards the pool of Lethe.

V. The nature of this lighter literature, and the changes which
it has undergone with the fashions of the last twenty years,
deserve consideration for many reasons, and afford a subject of
speculation which may be amusing, and I would add instructive,
were I not fearful of terrifying my readers in the outset. As
every age has its own character, manners, and amusements,
which are influenced even in their lightest forms by the funda-
mental features of the time, the moral and political character of
the age or nation may be read by an attentive observer even in
its lightest literature, how remote soever *prima facie* from morals
and politics.

VI. The newspaper of the day, the favourite magazine of the
month, the review of the quarter, the tour, the novel, and the
poem which are most recent in date and most fashionable in
name, furnish forth the morning table of the literary dilettante.
The spring tide of metropolitan favour floats these intellectual
deliciae into every minor town and village in the kingdom, where
they circle through their little day in the eddies of reading
societies.

VII. It may be questioned how far the favour of fashionable
readers is a criterion of literary merit. It is certain that no work

attracts any great share of general attention, which does not possess considerable originality and great power to interest and amuse. But originality will sometimes attract notice for a little space, as Mr Romeo Coates attracted some three or four audiences by the mere force of excessive absurdity: and the records of the Minerva press will shew that a considerable number of readers can be both interested and amused by works completely expurgated of all the higher qualities of mind. And without dragging reluctant dullness back to-day, let us only consider the names of Monk Lewis and of Kotzebue, from what acclamations of popular applause they have sunk in a few years into comparative oblivion, and we shall see that the condition of a fashionable author differs very little in stability from that of a political demagogue.

[VIII. Mr Walter Scott seems an exception to this. Having long occupied the poetical throne, he seems indeed to have been deposed by Lord Byron, but he has risen with redoubled might as a novelist, and has thus continued, from the publication of the *Lay of the Last Minstrel*, the most popular writer of his time; perhaps the most universally successful in his own day of any writer that ever lived. He has the rare talent of pleasing all ranks and classes of men, from the peer to the peasant, and all orders and degrees of mind from the philosopher to the man-milliner, of whom nine make a taylor. On the arrival of *Rob Roy*, as formerly on that of *Marmion*, the scholar lays aside his Plato, the statesman suspends his calculations, the young lady deserts her harp, the critic smiles as he trims his lamp, the lounger thanks God for his good fortune, and the weary artisan resigns his sleep for the refreshment of the magic page. But we must not anticipate.]

IX. Periodical publications form a very prominent feature in this transitory literature:—To any one who will compare the Reviews and Magazines of the present day with those of thirty years ago, it must be obvious that there is a much greater diffusion of general talent through them all, and more instances of great individual talent in the present than at the former period:

and at the same time it must be equally obvious that there is much less literary honesty, much more illiberality and exclusiveness, much more subdivision into petty gangs and factions, much less classicality and very much less philosophy. The stream of knowledge seems spread over a wider superficies, but what it has gained in breadth it has lost in depth. There is more dictionary learning, more scientific smattering, more of that kind of knowledge which is calculated for shew in general society, to produce a brilliant impression on the passing hour of literature, and less, far less, of that solid and laborious research which builds up in the silence of the closet, and in the disregard of perishable fashions of mind, the strong and permanent structure of history and philosophy.

x. The two principal periodical publications of the time—the *Edinburgh* and *Quarterly Reviews*—are the organs and oracles of the two great political factions, the Whigs and Tories; and their extensive circulation is less ascribable to any marked superiority, either of knowledge or talent, which they possess over their minor competitors, than to the curiosity of the public in general to learn or divine from these semi-official oracles what the said two factions are meditating.

xi. The *Quarterly Review* and the *Courier* newspaper are works conducted on the same principles and partly by the same contributors. These are the hardy veterans of corruption. The *British Critic*, the *Gentleman's Magazine*, and the [blank space in MS.] are its awkward squad: the *Anti-jacobin Review* and the *New Times* are its condemned regiment.

xii. The *country gentlemen*** appear to be in the habit of considering reviews as the joint productions of a body of men who meet at a sort of green board, where all new literary productions are laid before them for impartial consideration, and the merits of each having been fairy canvassed, some aged and enlightened censor records the opinion of the council and promulgates its

---

* A generic term applied by courtesy to the profoundly ignorant of all classes.

definitive judgment to the world. The solitary quack becomes a medical board. The solitary play-frequenter becomes a committee of amateurs of the drama. The elector of Old Sarum is a respectable body of constituents. This is an all-pervading quackery. Plurality is its essence. The mysterious *we* of the invisible assassin converts his poisoned dagger into a host of legitimate broadswords. Nothing, however, can be more remote from the facts. Of the ten or twelve articles which compose the *Edinburgh Review*, one is manufactured on the spot, another comes from Aberdeen, another from Islington, another from Herefordshire, another from the coast of Devon, another from bonny Dundee, *etc., etc., etc.,* without any one of the contributors even knowing the names of his brethren, or having any communication with any one but the editor. The only point of union among them is respect for the magic circle drawn by the compasses of faction and nationality, within which dullness and ignorance is secure of favour, and without which genius and knowledge are equally certain of neglect or persecution.

XIII. The case is much the same with the *Quarterly Review* except that the contributors are more in contact, being all more or less hired slaves of the Government, and for the most part gentlemen pensioners clustering round a common centre in the tangible shape of their paymaster Mr Gifford. This publication contains more talent and less principle than it would be easy to believe coexistent.

XIV. The monthly publications are so numerous that the most indefatigable reader of desultory literature could not get through the whole of their contents in a month: a very happy circumstance no doubt for that not innumerous class of persons who make the reading of reviews and magazines the sole business of their lives.

XV. All these have their own little exclusive circles of favour and faction, and it is very amusing to trace in any one of them half a dozen favoured names circling in the pre-eminence of glory in that little circle, and scarcely named or known out of it.

Glory, it is said, is like a circle in the water, that grows feebler and feebler as it recedes from the centre and expands with a wider circumference: but the glory of these little idols of little literary factions is like the many circles produced by the simultaneous splashing of a multitude of equal-sized pebbles, which each throws out for a few inches its own little series of concentric circles, limiting and limited by the small rings of its brother pebbles, [while in the midst of all this petty splashing in the pool of public favour Scott or Byron plunges a ponderous fragment in the centre and effaces them all with its eddy: but the disturbing power ceases: the splashings recommence, and the pebbles dance with joy in the rings of their self-created fame.]

xvi. Each of these little concentrations of genius has its own little audience of admirers, who, reading only those things which belong to their own party or gang, peep through these intellectual telescopes, and think they have a complete view of the age while they see only a minute fraction of it. Thus it fares with the insulated reader of a solitary review: the inhabitants of large towns, the frequenters of reading rooms, who consult them *en masse* [sentence unfinished in MS.]

xvii. In these publications, the mutual flattery of 'learned correspondents' to their own 'inestimable miscellany' carries the 'Tickle me, Mr Hayley' principle to a surprising extent.

xviii. There is a systematical cant in criticism which passes with many for the language of superior intelligence; such, for instance, is that which pronounces unintelligible whatever is in any degree obscure, more especially if it be really matter of deeper sense than the critic likes to be molested with. A critic is bound to study for an author's meaning, and not to make his own stupidity another's reproach. (The *Edinburgh Review* and *Excursion* and *Christabel*.)—How very ill Pindar would have fared with these gentlemen, we may readily imagine; nay, we have sufficiently seen, in the memorable instance in which he appeared *incognito* before a renowned Græculus of the critical corps.

xix. This instance occurred in an article on one of the most admirable pieces of philosophical criticism that has appeared in any language: Knight's *Principles of Taste*. One of the best metaphysical and one of the best moral treatises in our language appeared at the same time. The period seemed to promise the revival of philosophy: but it has since fallen into deeper sleep than ever, and even classical literature seems sinking into the same repose. The favourite journals of the day, only within a very few years, were seldom without a classical and a philosophical article for the grace of keeping up appearances: but now we have volume after volume without either, and almost without any thing to remind us that such things were.

xx. Sir William Drummond complains that philosophy is neglected at the universities from an exclusive respect for classical literature. I wish the reason were so good. Philosophy is discouraged from fear of itself, not from love of the classics. There would be too much philosophy in the latter for the purposes of public education, were it not happily neutralized by the very ingenious process of academical chemistry which separates reason from grammar, taste from prosody, philosophy from philology, and absorbs all perception of the charms of the former in tedium and disgust at the drudgery of the latter. Classical literature, thus disarmed of all power to shake the dominion of venerable mystery and hoary imposture, is used merely as a stepping-stone to church preferment, and there, God knows,

> Small skill in Latin and still less in Greek
> Is more than adequate to all we seek. —

xxi. If periodical criticism were honestly and conscientiously conducted, it might be a question how far it has been beneficial or injurious to literature: but being, as it is, merely a fraudulent and exclusive tool of party and partiality, that it is highly detrimental to it none but a trading critic will deny. The success of a new work is made to depend, in a great measure, not on the degree of its intrinsic merit, but on the degree of interest the publisher may have with the periodical press. Works of weight and utility, indeed, aided by the great counterpoise Time, break through these flimsy obstacles; but on the light and transient literature of the day its effect is almost omnipotent. Personal or political alliance being the only passports to critical notice, the independence and high thinking, that keeps an individual aloof from all the petty subdivisions of faction, makes every several gang his foe: and of this the *late* Mr Wordsworth is a striking example.

XXII. There is a common influence to which the periodical press is subservient: it has many ultras on the side of power, but none on the side of liberty (one or two *weekly* publications excepted). And this is not from want of sufficient liberty of the press, which is ample to all purposes; it is from want of an audience. There is a degree of spurious liberty, a Whiggish moderation with which many will go hand in hand; but few have the courage to push enquiry to its limits.

XXIII. Now though there is no censorship of the press, there is an influence widely diffused and mighty in its operation that is almost equivalent to it. The whole scheme of our government is based in influence, and the immense number of genteel persons, who are maintained by the taxes, gives this influence an extent and complication from which few persons are free. They shrink from truth, for it shews those dangers which they dare not face. The *legatur* of corruption must be stamped upon a work before it can be admitted to fashionable circulation.

XXIV. In orthodox families that have the advantage of being acquainted with such a phænomenon as a reading parson (which is fortunately as rare as the Atropos Belladonna—a hunting parson, on the other hand, a much more innocent variety, being as common as the Solanum Nigrum) or any tolerably literate variety of political and theological orthodoxy—the reading of the young ladies is very much influenced by his advice. He is careful not to prohibit, unless in extreme cases—Voltaire, for example—who is by many well-meaning grown ladies and gentlemen in leading-strings considered little better than a devil incarnate. He is careful not to prohibit, for prohibition is usually accompanied with longing for forbidden fruit—it is much more easy to exclude by silence, and pre-occupy by counter-recommendation. Young ladies read only for amusement: the best recommendation a work of fancy can have is that it should inculcate no opinions at all, but implicitly acquiesce in all the assumptions of worldly wisdom. The next best is that it should be well-seasoned with *petitiones principii* in favour of things as they are.

xxv. Fancy indeed treads on dangerous ground when she trespasses on the land of opinion—the soil is too slippery for her glass slippers, and the atmosphere too heavy for her filmy wings. But she is a degenerate spirit if she be contented within the limits of her own empire, and keep the mind continually gazing upon phantasms without pointing to more important realities. Her province is to awaken the mind, not to enchain it. Poetry precedes philosophy, but true poetry prepares its path. See Forsyth.

xxvi. Cervantes, Rabelais, Swift, Voltaire, Fielding have led fancy against opinion with a success that no other names can parallel. Works of mere amusement, that teach nothing, may have an accidental and transient success, but cannot of course have influence on their own times, and will certainly not pass to posterity. Mr Scott's success has been attributed in a great measure to his keeping clear of opinion. [But he is far from being a writer who teaches nothing. On the contrary, he communicates great and valuable information. He is a painter of manners. He is the historian of a peculiar and remote class of our own countrymen, who within a few years have completely passed away. He offers materials to the philosopher in depicting, with the truth of life, the features of human nature in a peculiar state of society, before comparatively little known.]

xxvii. Information, not enquiry—manners, not morals—facts, not inferences—are the taste of the present day. If philosophy be not dead, she is at least sleeping in the country of Bacon and Locke. The seats of learning (as the universities are still called, according to the proverb, 'Once a captain always a captain') are armed *cap-à-pie* against her. The metaphysician, having lifted his voice and been regarded by no man, folds up his Plato and writes a poem.

XXVIII. The article of the Edinburgh Reviewers on Mr Coleridge's *Christabel* affords a complete specimen of the manner in which criticism is now conducted, and certainly nothing but the most implicit contempt for their readers, and the most absolute reliance on the prostration of public judgment before the throne of criticism, could have induced them to put forth such a tissue of ignorance, folly, and *fraud*. The last is a grave charge, but it is the worst and the most prominent feature of modern criticism: for as to ignorance and folly, they are by no means criminal, and are perhaps indispensable in critical journals, for whose *non integra lignea* wisdom and learning would be too heavy ballast. But neither ignorance nor folly, nor any thing but the most unblushing fraud, could have dictated the following passage. *Crimine ab uno disce omnes.*

[It is obvious that at this point—though his MS. supplies neither quotation nor reference—Peacock intended to insert the following passage from the *Edinburgh Review* for September, 1816, Vol. XXVII, p. 64.]

> One word as to the metre of Christabel, or, as Mr Coleridge terms it, '*the* Christabel'—happily enough; for indeed we doubt if the peculiar force of the definite article was ever more strongly exemplified. He says, that though the reader may fancy there prevails a great *irregularity* in the metre, some lines being of four, others of twelve syllables, yet in reality it is quite regular; only that it is 'founded on a new principle, namely, that of counting in each line the accents, not the syllables'. We say nothing of the monstrous assurance of any man coming forward coolly at this time of day, and telling the readers of English poetry, whose ear has been tuned to the lays of Spenser, Milton, Dryden, and Pope, that he makes his metre 'on a new principle!' but we utterly deny the truth of the assertion, and defy him to show us *any* principle upon which his lines can be conceived to tally. We give two or three specimens, to confound at once this miserable piece of cox-combry and shuffling. Let our 'wild, and singularly original and

beautiful' author, show us how these lines agree either in number of accents or of feet.

> 'Ah wel-a-day!' —
>
> 'For this is alone in —'
>
> 'And didst bring her home with thee in love and in charity' —
>
> 'I pray you drink this cordial wine' —
>
> 'Sir Leoline' —
>
> 'And found a bright lady surpassingly fair' —
>
> 'Tu—whit!——Tu—whoo!'

Now Mr Coleridge expressly says: Though the syllables may vary from *seven* to *twelve* the number of accents will be found always the same: *i.e.* four. If the reviewer had had the common candour which characterizes even the lowest of mankind (reviewers excepted), he would have stated Mr Coleridge's assertion truly, and then have disproved it if it had appeared erroneous. Mr Coleridge asserts that lines of any number of syllables from seven to twelve contain alike four accents, and [nothing can be more] true: and how does the reviewer disprove this assertion: He first omits the limitation, and makes him say what he never said, that all his lines contain the same number of accents; and then placing lines of four and fourteen syllables in contact. Can any one suppose that the suppression was not wilful? That a man would copy one half of a sentence, the whole of which he could not disprove, and argue against the half as if it were the whole? Could any man do this under any supposition but that of wilful and fraudulent misrepresentation? Or would any man have ventured to do it if he had not felt conscious that in his capacity of critical purveyor he was catering not for liberality and taste but for envy and malignity?

xxix. Reviews have been published in this country seventy years: eight hundred and forty months: and if we reckon only on an average four numbers to a month, we shall find that in that period three thousand three hundred and sixty numbers have been published:* three thousand three hundred and sixty numbers, two hundred thousand pages, of sheer criticism, every

---

* This excludes magazines.

page of which is now in existence. What a treasury of information! What a repertory of excellent jokes to be cracked on an unhappy author and his unfavoured publications! So it would seem. Yet on examination these excellent jokes reduce themselves to some half dozen, which have been repeated through every number of every review of the bulk of periodical criticism to the present day (and were stale in the first instance), without apparently losing any portion of what Miss Edgeworth would call the raciness of their humour. They were borrowed in the first instance from Pope, who himself took one or two of them at second hand. They have an everlasting gloss, like the three coats in the *Tale of a Tub*.

xxx. One of these is the profundity of the Bathos. There is in the lowest deep a lower still, and the author in question (be he who he may) has plunged lower than any one before him. Another is that the work in question is a narcotic, and sets the unfortunate critic to sleep. A third is that it is unintelligible, and that true no-meaning puzzles more than wit. A fourth, that the author is insane. It cannot be denied that this is super-excellent wit which can bear so much repetition without palling, for there is not any number of any review which does not contain them all at least once, and sometimes six or seven times: but taking them only at an average of one in a number, they have been repeated three thousand three hundred and sixty times in seventy years, and so far it is demonstrated that they are three thousand three hundred and sixty times better than the best joke in Joseph Miller, whose brightest recorded repartees will not bear a second repetition.

xxxi. This ready cut and dried wit, thus stamped with eternal currency, is very convenient to a trading critic who has no wit of his own; and when all this mighty artillery is concentrated in a single article, the great hand of fulminating Jove is armed with a thunderbolt indeed. *Tres imbris torti radios, etc.* The reviewer of *Christabel* accordingly has seized them all, and launched them at the devoted head of his Capaneus, Mr Coleridge (three extracts and parallel notes).

XXXII. Lord Byron had, it seems, in a singularly original collocation of words, characterized Christabel as a 'wild and singularly original and beautiful poem'. This unfortunate phrase proved a tid-bit for the critics, who rung the changes upon it with infinite whim.

> ' 'Tis the middle of night by the castle clock,
> And the owls have awaken'd the crowing cock;
> Tu—whit!——Tu—whoo!
> And hark, again! the crowing cock,
> How drowsily it crew.'
> 'Sir Leoline, the Baron rich,
> Hath a toothless mastiff bitch;
> From her kennel beneath the rock
> She makes answer to the clock,
> Four for the quarters, and twelve for the hour;
> Ever and aye, moonshine or shower,
> Sixteen short howls, not over loud;
> Some say she sees my lady's shroud.'
> 'Is the night chilly and dark?
> The night is chilly, but not dark.'

It is probable that Lord Byron may have had this passage in his eye, when he called the poem 'wild' and 'original'; but how he discovered it to be 'beautiful', is not quite so easy for us to imagine.

The critic does not condescend to alledge any reason for his disapprobation: he knew well that his readers would not require any, but on his magisterial affirmation would take it for granted that the passage was naught, without exercising a grain of judgment for themselves.—But with all due deference to this Aristarchus, let us examine the culprit on whom he thus summarily pronounces. Christabel is a ballad romance, a tale of wonder and mystery told with the simplicity of our elder minstrels, who depict every scene as it were passing under their eyes, and narrate their most marvellous legends with an unaffected *bonne foi*, that shews a mind fully impressed with the truth of its own tale. They never destroyed the appearance of self-persuasion by too much minuteness of detail, and a perpetual pausing to explain and account for every thing. They seem to tell us much as they know, and leave it to be supposed that there is much more of which they are ignorant. Their language is always that of circumstantial evidence, never of complete and positive testimony. (Note. *Sir Patrick Spence*.) Their style is at once simple and energetic, unincumbered with extraneous ornaments; the natural expression of distinctly conceived imagery, rising and falling with the elevation or homeliness of the subject. Such is the style and the language of *Christabel*. The poet relates a tale of magic and mystery, as one who is himself perplexed by the dark wonders which have passed under his own knowledge. The poem is a succession of scenes, and every succession or change presents as many visible or audible circumstances as the fancy can comprehend at once without vacancy from their fewness or confusion from their multitude (note Homer Milton *etc.* as opposed to Chaucer and his modern imitators.) The first scene, the castle at midnight, is characterized by a few circumstances at once original and true to nature. And the regular howl of the dog, under some unknown supernatural influence, prepares the reader at once for a supernatural tale.

> Much of the art of the wild writers consists in sudden transitions—opening eagerly upon some topic, and then flying from it immediately. This indeed is known to the medical men, who not unfrequently have the care of them, as an unerring symptom. Accordingly, here we take leave of the Mastiff Bitch, and lose sight of her entirely, upon the entrance of another personage of a higher degree,
>> 'The lovely Lady Christabel,
>> Whom her father loves so well'

This short sentence is admirable in many ways. We have the three thousand three hundred and sixtieth repetition of the fourth standard joke, which insinuates that the author is insane; and secondly, a profound discovery that all poetry is mad that is not monodramatical, and that any person or object, once brought on the stage, must remain in constant view to the end without being displaced by any other; and that consequently

Shakespeare in his *Macbeth*, having eagerly opened upon three witches, and made us immediately lose sight of them on the entrance of another personage of a higher degree, King Duncan, thereby gave an unerring symptom that he ought to have been forthwith consigned to the care of Doctor Monro.

'The lovely lady Christabel...' who it seems had been rambling about all night.

The poem neither says nor implies any such thing. Christabel has just left the castle and walked into the wood. Extract from the poem: then from the criticism.

With 'the key that fitted well': the expression Homeric: note on '*I wis*' and '*all* in the middle of the gate': Lady G. then sinks down ' "belike through pain"; but it should seem more probably from laziness.' This is misrepresentation again: Geraldine is a witch who designs evil to Christabel: this is obvious enough throughout: she cannot pass the threshold of the castle, nor afterwards of Christabel's apartment, unless Christabel herself be the agent of her transition *(Eve of St John, etc.)* —She therefore in both instances sinks down on the threshold apparently from weariness (The poet says 'belike through weariness' in the character of one who sees the action and does but guess at its cause) and Christabel, so interpreting it, lifts her over it. She then walks on as she were not in pain: implying that the conjecture 'belike through weariness' was unfounded. The supernatural powers of Geraldine, the evil which she intends to Christabel, *etc., etc.,* are always told by implication: the whole effect of the poem would be destroyed were they told in any other manner... 'too much tired to speak'— ?...It is the implication of a charmed sleep, and of the consciousness on the part of the sleeping dog of the presence of an evil guest. The critic could scarcely be so stupid as not to see this, but it is wonderful how far a little understanding can be wholly darkened when its whole attention is directed, not to understand a work, but to disparage and misrepresent it...'a dram of some home-made liquor...'

> 'O weary lady, Geraldine,
> I pray you, drink this cordial wine!
> It is a wine of virtuous powers;
> My mother made it of wild flowers...'

now would this passage to any but a genuine and *bona fide* gar-
reteer capable of pawning the very book he was reviewing for a
glass of brandy—have suggested any such idea as that of com-
forting themselves with a dram!

> 'Like a lady of a far countree'...from which we may gather among
> other points the exceeding great beauty of all women who live in a
> distant place, no matter where.

The true meaning of the passage is obvious: she was most
beautiful *and* had the air of a foreigner. The conjunction was
superfluous and would have marred the passage, without check-
ing the critic's predetermined ridicule: for this species of wit is
the cheapest of all, and can find abundant food in the most perfect compositions, as we shall presently shew.

> —a very dark spell, which we apprehend the poet manufactured
> by shaking words together at random; for it is impossible to fancy
> that he can annex any meaning whatever to it.

Here we have the third standard joke, that the passage is unintelligible: but the critic has shot his bolt too soon, according to
the proverb, for the passage is scarcely obscure, and is indeed
intelligible to the meanest capacity, though seriously perhaps
not to our reviewer's. This is the whole of it. Explain it.

'To understand what follows, we own, surpasses our comprehension.' The third standard joke again... 'The Baron falls
into a passion, as if he had discovered that his daughter had been
seduced; at least, we can understand him in no other sense,
though no hint of such a kind is given; but, on the contrary, she
is painted to the last moment as full of innocence and purity.
Nevertheless,

> "His heart was cleft with pain and rage,
> His cheeks they quiver'd, his eyes were wild,
> Dishonour'd thus in his old age;
> Dishonour'd by his only child;

> And all his hospitality
> To th' insulted daughter of his friend
> By more than woman's jealousy,
> Brought thus to a disgraceful end—" '

Surely none but an idiot could truly misunderstand this, and yet I am inclined to take the critic at his word, and believe that he really did; but the meaning is manifest. Christabel brings the Lady Geraldine and tells him all that it is in her power to declare, *etc.*, thus recommending her to the baron's hospitality, and shortly after, without any obvious reason, desires him to send the woman away. The Baron's heart is cleft with rage for the disgrace thus brought upon his hospitality, which was the chief of virtues in those days: he is dishonoured in his old age by his daughter's violation of hospitality: he attributes this to jealousy of the parental kindness with which he had received the daughter of his friend, and which, if it had been Christabel's true motive, would have been indeed more than woman's jealousy, and therefore—extr:

I blush for an age of literature in which any one can require an explanation of so plain a sentence; still more for an age in which any one can come forward and tell the public that, in the grovelling stupidity of his intellect, he cannot understand what is intelligible to a child, and that for this very declaration he shall be held an oracle. Truly this is like what Locke tells us of Egypt, where complete and incurable idiocy is a title to divine honours.

> Nothing further is said to explain the mystery; but there follows incontinently, what is termed '*The conclusion of Part the Second*'. And as we are pretty confident that Mr Coleridge holds this passage in the highest estimation; that he prizes it more than any other part of 'that wild, and singularly original and beautiful poem Christabel', excepting always the two passages touching the 'toothless mastiff Bitch'; we shall extract it for the amazement of our readers—premising our own frank avowal that we are wholly unable to divine that meaning of any portion of it.

The third standard joke for the third time.

'A little child, a limber elf,
Singing, dancing to itself,
A fairy thing with red round cheeks,
That always finds and never seeks;
Makes such a vision to the sight
As fills a father's eyes with light;
And pleasures flow in so thick and fast
Upon his heart, that he at last
Must needs express his love's excess
With words of unmeant bitterness.
Perhaps 'tis pretty to force together
Thoughts so all unlike each other;
To mutter and mock a broken charm,
To dally with wrong that does no harm.
Perhaps 'tis tender too, and pretty,
At each wild word to feel within
A sweet recoil of love and pity.
And what if in a world of sin
(O sorrow and shame should this be true!)
Such giddiness of heart and brain
Comes seldom save from rage and pain,
So talks as it's most used to do.'

Obscure this probably is—unintelligible it is not—at all events the meaning of portions of it is sufficiently plain.

'A little child' *etc.* down to 'light'.

So far there is no difficulty to any one but our reviewer.

'And pleasures—bitterness—'

The meaning is still obvious, though the fact may be questioned that a father, contemplating his playful child, will experience pleasure so excessive that the ordinary language of pleasure cannot express it, and he therefore of necessity borrows the language of bitterness to express the excess of his love. So far as the use of such terms 'little lovely rascal' *etc.* this is certainly true.

'Perhaps 'tis pretty to force together' *etc.*
'To dally with wrong that does no harm.'

which is certainly the case when excessive affection prompts the employment of such language.

> 'Perhaps 'tis tender too, and pretty,' to 'pity'.

As if there were an injustice in employing such terms at all, though the language of ordinary affection can find none sufficiently forcible.

> 'And what if in a world of sin' *etc.*

The fact that words of bitterness are often employed to express excessive affection being assumed, the cause is then surmised: The state of excessive love and delight is a giddiness of heart and brain. But in a world of sin, giddiness of heart and brain is caused more frequently by pain and rage than by love and delight. Therefore when the state of giddiness *etc.*, which is a habit of pain and rage, occurs from its less frequent cause of love and delight, it employs the language of its more frequent habit, and talks as it is most used to do.

The fact may be denied, and if the fact be admitted the solution may be controverted: but the poet's meaning is clear, and the critic who proclaims his own inability to comprehend it, comes forward like Dogberry, and gravely intreats to be written down an ass: and indeed if the voluntary confession of stupidity were in those days, as in ours, the passport to reputation for extraordinary critical acumen and judicial sagacity, honest Dogberry's desire is by no means ridiculous.

> 'A damsel with a dulcimer
> In a vision once I saw:
> It was an Abyssinian maid
> And on her dulcimer she play'd,
> Singing of Mount Abora.
> Could I revive within me
> Her symphony and song,
> To such a deep delight 'twould win me,
> That with music loud and long,
> I would build that dome in air,
> That sunny dome! those caves of ice!

> And all who heard should see them there,
> And all should cry, Beware! Beware!
> His flashing eyes, his floating hair!
> Weave a circle round him thrice,
> And close your eyes with holy dread:
> For he on honey-dew hath fed.'

It is extremely probable that Mr Coleridge, being a very visionary gentleman, has somewhat deceived himself respecting the origin of *Kubla Khan*; and as the story of its having been composed in his sleep must necessarily, by all who are acquainted with his manner of narrating matter of fact, be received with a certain degree of scepticism, its value as a psychological curiosity is nothing, and whatever value it has is in its poetic merit alone. But from its having been asserted by the author to have been produced in sleep, it was to be foreseen that the third standard joke would present itself to the critics too naturally to be passed by; that the poem itself would be pronounced to be a narcotic, and to smell strongly of the anodyne, *etc. etc.*; and accordingly, in every review which I have seen of *Christabel*, this very exquisite joke has been duly cracked over the head of *Kubla Khan*. It has been uniformly pronounced unintelligible, especially that passage beginning 'a damsel with a dulcimer' *etc*. As the poem is short, and the manner in which the critics have treated it affords throughout an excellent standard of critical taste and sagacity, I will insert the whole of it, prefixing a number to each sentence as a reference to the following observations.

> In Xanadu did Kubla Khan
> A stately pleasure-dome decree:
> Where Alph, the sacred river, ran
> Through caverns measureless to man
>   Down to a sunless sea.

I have read this poem several times over to discover what is unintelligible in it, as intending to explain it for the benefit of the critics, in the hope that when they have got their lesson, and learned to understand it, some of them will condescend to tell us anew what they think of it. For that a man should pass judgment without understanding what is in itself intelligible, is as if a judge should take a nap during the latter half of [a] trial, and waking to give his charge should say to the jury: 'Gentlemen, I do not understand the defendant's evidence; therefore you will do well to find for the plaintiff.' The jury, if not a special jury, would naturally say, 'My lord, if you do not understand the evidence, we do; and are therefore better qualified to give judgment on it than your lordship.' I do not believe that to any person of ordinary comprehension, who will take the pains to read this poem twice over, there will appear any thing unintelligible or incoherent in it: indeed there are very few specimens of lyrical poetry so plain, so consistent, so completely *simplex et unum* from first to last.

THE
FOUR AGES OF
POETRY

THE FOUR AGES OF POETRY

Qui inter haec nutriuntur non magis sapere possunt, quam bene olere qui in culina habitant. PETRONIUS.

POETRY, like the world, may be said to have four ages, but in a different order: the first age of poetry being the age of iron; the second, of gold; the third, of silver; and the fourth, of brass.

The first, or iron age of poetry, is that in which rude bards celebrate in rough numbers the exploits of ruder chiefs, in days when every man is a warrior, and when the great practical maxim of every form of society, 'to keep what we have and to catch what we can', is not yet disguised under names of justice and forms of law, but is the naked motto of the naked sword, which is the only judge and jury in every question of *meum* and *tuum*. In these days, the only three trades flourishing (besides that of priest which flourishes always) are those of king, thief, and beggar: the beggar being for the most part a king deject, and the thief a king expectant. The first question asked of a stranger is, whether he is a beggar or a thief:* the stranger, in reply, usually assumes the first, and waits a convenient opportunity to prove his claim to the second appellation.

The natural desire of every man to engross to himself as much power and property as he can acquire by any of the means which might makes right, is accompanied by the no less natural desire of making known to as many people as possible the extent to which he has been a winner in this universal game. The successful warrior becomes a chief; the successful chief becomes a

---

* See the *Odyssey*, passim; and Thucydides, 1. 5.

king: his next want is an organ to disseminate the fame of his
achievements and the extent of his possessions; and this organ
he finds in a bard, who is always ready to celebrate the strength
of his arm, being first duly inspired by that of his liquor. This
is the origin of poetry, which, like all other trades, takes its rise
in the demand for the commodity, and flourishes in proportion
to the extent of the market.

Poetry is thus in its origin panegyrical. The first rude songs
of all nations appear to be a sort of brief historical notices, in a
strain of tumid hyperbole, of the exploits and possessions of a
few pre-eminent individuals. They tell us how many battles
such an one has fought, how many helmets he has cleft, how
many breastplates he has pierced, how many widows he has
made, how much land he has appropriated, how many houses
he has demolished for other people, what a large one he has
built for himself, how much gold he has stowed away in it, and
how liberally and plentifully he pays, feeds, and intoxicates the
divine and immortal bards, the sons of Jupiter, but for whose
everlasting songs the names of heroes would perish.

This is the first stage of poetry before the invention of written
letters. The numerical modulation is at once useful as a help to
memory, and pleasant to the ears of uncultured men, who are
easily caught by sound: and from the exceeding flexibility of the
yet unformed language, the poet does no violence to his ideas
in subjecting them to the fetters of number. The savage indeed
lisps in numbers, and all rude and uncivilized people express
themselves in the manner which we call poetical.

The scenery by which he is surrounded, and the superstitions which are the creed of his age, form the poet's mind.
Rocks, mountains, seas, unsubdued forests, unnavigable rivers,
surround him with forms of power and mystery, which ignorance and fear have peopled with spirits, under multifarious
names of gods, goddesses, nymphs, genii, and dæmons. Of all
these personages marvellous tales are in existence: the nymphs
are not indifferent to handsome young men, and the gentlemen-
genii are much troubled and very troublesome with a propen-

sity to be rude to pretty maidens: the bard therefore finds no
difficulty in tracing the genealogy of his chief to any of the deities
in his neighbourhood with whom the said chief may be most
desirous of claiming relationship.

In this pursuit, as in all others, some of course will attain a
very marked pre-eminence; and these will be held in high
honour, like Demodocus in the *Odyssey*, and will be consequently
inflated with boundless vanity, like Thamyris in the *Iliad*. Poets
are as yet the only historians and chroniclers of their time, and
the sole depositories of all the knowledge of their age; and
though this knowledge is rather a crude congeries of traditional
phantasies than a collection of useful truths, yet, such as it is,
they have it to themselves. They are observing and thinking,
while others are robbing and fighting: and though their object
be nothing more than to secure a share of the spoil, yet they
accomplish this end by intellectual, not by physical, power:
their success excites emulation to the attainment of intellectual
eminence: thus they sharpen their own wits and awaken those
of others, at the same time that they gratify vanity and amuse
curiosity. A skilful display of the little knowledge they have,
gains them credit for the possession of much more which they
have not. Their familiarity with the secret history of gods and
genii obtains for them, without much difficulty, the reputation
of inspiration; thus they are not only historians but theologians,
moralists, and legislators: delivering their oracles *ex cathedra*,
and being indeed often themselves (as Orpheus and Amphion)
regarded as portions and emanations of divinity: building cities
with a song, and leading brutes with a symphony; which are only
metaphors for the faculty of leading multitudes by the nose.

The golden age of poetry finds its materials in the age of iron.
This age begins when poetry begins to be retrospective; when
something like a more extended system of civil polity is established; when personal strength and courage avail less to the
aggrandizing of their possessor and to the making and marring
of kings and kingdoms, and are checked by organized bodies,
social institutions, and hereditary successions. Men also live

more in the light of truth and within the interchange of observation; and thus perceive that the agency of gods and genii is
not so frequent among themselves as, to judge from the songs
and legends of past time, it was among their ancestors. From
these two circumstances, really diminished personal power,
and apparently diminished familiarity with gods and genii, they
very easily and naturally deduce two conclusions: 1st, That men
are degenerated, and 2nd, That they are less in favour with the
gods. The people of the petty states and colonies, which have
now acquired stability and form, which owed their origin and
first prosperity to the talents and courage of a single chief,
magnify their founder through the mists of distance and tradition, and perceive him achieving wonders with a god or goddess
at his elbow. They find his name and his exploits thus magnified
and accompanied in their traditionary songs, which are their
only memorials. All that is said of him is in this character.
There is nothing to contradict it. The man and his exploits and
his tutelary deities are mixed and blended in one invariable
association. The marvellous too is very much like a snow-ball:
it grows as it rolls downward, till the little nucleus of truth
which began its descent from the summit is hidden in the
accumulation of super-induced hyperbole.

When tradition, thus adorned and exaggerated, has surrounded the founders of families and states with so much adven-
titious power and magnificence, there is no praise which a living
poet can, without fear of being kicked for clumsy flattery,
address to a living chief, that will not still leave the impression
that the latter is not so great a man as his ancestors. The man
must in this case be praised through his ancestors. Their greatness must be established, and he must be shown to be their
worthy descendant. All the people of a state are interested in
the founder of their state. All states that have harmonized into
a common form of society, are interested in their respective
founders. All men are interested in their ancestors. All men
love to look back into the days that are past. In these circumstances traditional national poetry is reconstructed and brought

like chaos into order and form. The interest is more universal: understanding is enlarged: passion still has scope and play: character is still various and strong: nature is still unsubdued and existing in all her beauty and magnificence, and men are not yet excluded from her observation by the magnitude of cities or the daily confinement of civic life: poetry is more an art: it requires greater skill in numbers, greater command of language, more extensive and various knowledge, and greater comprehensiveness of mind. It still exists without rivals in any other department of literature; and even the arts, painting and sculpture certainly, and music probably, are comparatively rude and imperfect. The whole field of intellect is its own. It has no rivals in history, nor in philosophy, nor in science. It is cultivated by the greatest intellects of the age, and listened to by all the rest. This is the age of Homer, the golden age of poetry. Poetry has now attained its perfection: it has attained the point which it cannot pass: genius therefore seeks new forms for the treatment of the same subjects: hence the lyric poetry of Pindar and Alcaeus, and the tragic poetry of Aeschylus and Sophocles. The favour of kings, the honour of the Olympic crown, the applause of present multitudes, all that can feed vanity and stimulate rivalry, await the successful cultivator of this art, till its forms become exhausted, and new rivals arise around it in new fields of literature, which gradually acquire more influence as, with the progress of reason and civilization, facts become more interesting than fiction: indeed the maturity of poetry may be considered the infancy of history. The transition from Homer to Herodotus is scarcely more remarkable than that from Herodotus to Thucydides: in the gradual dereliction of fabulous incident and ornamented language, Herodotus is as much a poet in relation to Thucydides as Homer is in relation to Herodotus. The history of Herodotus is half a poem: it was written while the whole field of literature yet belonged to the Muses, and the nine books of which it was composed were therefore of right, as well as courtesy, superinscribed with their nine names.

Speculations, too, and disputes, on the nature of man and of mind; on moral duties and on good and evil; on the animate and inanimate components of the visible world; begin to share attention with the eggs of Leda and the horns of Io, and to draw off from poetry a portion of its once undivided audience.

Then comes the silver age, or the poetry of civilized life. This poetry is of two kinds, imitative and original. The imitative consists in recasting, and giving an exquisite polish to, the poetry of the age of gold: of this Virgil is the most obvious and striking example. The original is chiefly comic, didactic, or satiric: as in Menander, Aristophanes, Horace, and Juvenal. The poetry of this age is characterized by an exquisite and fastidious selection of words, and a laboured and somewhat monotonous harmony of expression: but its monotony consists in this, that experience having exhausted all the varieties of modulation, the civilized poetry selects the most beautiful, and prefers the repetition of these to ranging through the variety of all. But the best expression being that into which the idea naturally falls, it requires the utmost labour and care so to reconcile the inflexibility of civilized language and the laboured polish of versification with the idea intended to be expressed, that sense may not appear to be sacrificed to sound. Hence numerous efforts and rare success.

This state of poetry is however a step towards its extinction. Feeling and passion are best painted in, and roused by, ornamental and figurative language; but the reason and the understanding are best addressed in the simplest and most unvarnished phrase. Pure reason and dispassionate truth would be perfectly ridiculous in verse, as we may judge by versifying one of Euclid's demonstrations. This will be found true of all dispassionate reasoning whatever, and of all reasoning that requires comprehensive views and enlarged combinations. It is only the more tangible points of morality, those which command assent at once, those which have a mirror in every mind, and in which the severity of reason is warmed and rendered palatable by being mixed up with feeling and imagination, that are applicable even to what is called moral poetry: and as the sciences of morals and of mind advance towards perfection, as they become more enlarged and comprehensive in their views, as reason gains the ascendancy in them over imagination and feeling, poetry can no longer accompany them in their progress, but drops into the background, and leaves them to advance alone.

Thus the empire of thought is withdrawn from poetry, as the empire of facts had been before. In respect of the latter, the poet of the age of iron celebrates the achievements of his contemporaries; the poet of the age of gold celebrates the heroes of the age of iron; the poet of the age of silver re-casts the poems of the age of gold: we may here see how very slight a ray of historical truth is sufficient to dissipate all the illusions of poetry. We know no more of the men than of the gods of the *Iliad*; no more of Achilles than we do of Thetis; no more of Hector and Andromache than we do of Vulcan and Venus: these belong altogether to poetry; history has no share in them: but Virgil knew better than to write an epic about Caesar; he left him to Livy; and travelled out of the confines of truth and history into the old regions of poetry and fiction.

Good sense and elegant learning, conveyed in polished and somewhat monotonous verse, are the perfection of the original and imitative poetry of civilized life. Its range is limited, and when exhausted, nothing remains but the *crambe repetita* of common-place, which at length becomes thoroughly wearisome, even to the most indefatigable readers of the newest new nothings.

It is now evident that poetry must either cease to be cultivated, or strike into a new path. The poets of the age of gold have been imitated and repeated till no new imitation will attract notice: the limited range of ethical and didactic poetry is exhausted: the associations of daily life in an advanced state of society are of very dry, methodical, unpoetical matters-of-fact: but there is always a multitude of listless idlers, yawning for amusement, and gaping for novelty: and the poet makes it his glory to be foremost among their purveyors.

Then comes the age of brass, which, by rejecting the polish and the learning of the age of silver, and taking a retrograde stride to the barbarisms and crude traditions of the age of iron, professes to return to nature and revive the age of gold. This is the second childhood of poetry. To the comprehensive energy of the Homeric Muse, which, by giving at once the grand outline of things, presented to the mind a vivid picture in one or two verses, inimitable alike in simplicity and magnificence, is substituted a verbose and minutely-detailed description of thoughts, passions, actions, persons, and things, in that loose rambling style of verse, which any one may write, *stans pede in uno*, at the rate of two hundred lines in an hour. To this age may be referred all the poets who flourished in the decline of the Roman Empire. The best specimen of it, though not the most generally known, is the *Dionysiaca* of Nonnus, which contains many passages of exceeding beauty in the midst of masses of amplification and repetition.

The iron age of classical poetry may be called the bardic; the golden, the Homeric; the silver, the Virgilian; and the brass, the Nonnic.

Modern poetry has also its four ages; but 'it wears its rue with a difference'.

To the age of brass in the ancient world succeeded the dark ages, in which the light of the Gospel began to spread over Europe, and in which, by a mysterious and inscrutable dispensation, the darkness thickened with the progress of the light, The tribes that overran the Roman Empire brought back the days of barbarism, but with this difference, that there were many books in the world, many places in which they were preserved, and occasionally some one by whom they were read, who indeed (if he escaped being burned *pour l'amour de Dieu*,) generally lived an object of mysterious fear, with the reputation of magician, alchymist, and astrologer. The emerging of the nations of Europe from this superinduced barbarism, and their settling into new forms of polity, was accompanied, as the first ages of Greece had been, with a wild spirit of adventure, which, co-operating with new manners and new superstitions, raised up a fresh crop of chimæras, not less fruitful, though far less beautiful, than those of Greece. The semi-deification of women by the maxims of the age of chivalry, combining with these new fables, produced the romance of the middle ages. The founders of the new line of heroes took the place of the demi-gods of Grecian poetry. Charlemagne and his Paladins, Arthur and his knights of the round table, the heroes of the iron age of chivalrous poetry, were seen through the same magnifying mist of distance, and their exploits were celebrated with even more extravagant hyperbole. These legends, combined with the exaggerated love that pervades the songs of the troubadours, the reputation of magic that attached to learned men, the infant wonders of natural philosophy, the crazy fanaticism of the crusades, the power and privileges of the great feudal chiefs, and the holy mysteries of monks and nuns, formed a state of society in which no two laymen could meet without fighting, and in which the three staple ingredients of lover, prize-fighter, and fanatic, that composed the basis of the character of every true man, were mixed up and diversified, in different individuals and classes, with so many distinctive excellencies, and under such an infinite motley variety of costume, as gave the range of a most extensive and picturesque field to the two great constituents of poetry, love and battle.

From these ingredients of the iron age of modern poetry, dispersed in the rhymes of minstrels and the songs of the troubadours, arose the golden age, in which the scattered materials were harmonized and blended about the time of the revival of learning; but with this peculiar difference, that Greek and Roman literature pervaded all the poetry of the golden age of modern poetry, and hence resulted a heterogeneous compound of all ages and nations in one picture; an infinite licence, which gave to the poet the free range of the whole field of imagination and memory. This was carried very far by Ariosto, but farthest of all by Shakespeare and his contemporaries, who used time and locality merely because they could not do without them, because every action must have its when and where: but they made no scruple of deposing a Roman Emperor by an Italian Count, and sending him off in the disguise of a French pilgrim to be shot with a blunderbuss by an English archer. This makes the old English drama very picturesque, at any rate, in the variety of costume, and very diversified in action and character; though it is a picture of nothing that ever was seen on earth except a Venetian carnival.

The greatest of English poets, Milton, may be said to stand alone between the ages of gold and silver, combining the excellencies of both; for with all the energy, and power, and freshness of the first, he united all the studied and elaborate magnificence of the second.

The silver age succeeded: beginning with Dryden, coming in perfection with Pope, and ending with Goldsmith, Collins, and Gray.

Cowper divested verse of its exquisite polish; he thought to metre, but paid more attention to his thoughts than his verse. It would be difficult to draw the boundary of prose and blank verse between his letters and his poetry.

The silver age was the reign of authority; but authority now began to be shaken, not only in poetry but in the whole sphere of its dominion. The contemporaries of Gray and Cowper were deep and elaborate thinkers. The subtle scepticism of Hume, the solemn irony of Gibbon, the daring paradoxes of Rousseau, and the biting ridicule of Voltaire, directed the energies of four extraordinary minds to shake every portion of the reign of authority. Enquiry was roused, the activity of intellect was excited, and poetry came in for its share of the general result. The changes had been rung on lovely maid and sylvan shade, summer heat and green retreat, waving trees and sighing breeze, gentle swains and amorous pains, by versifiers who took them on trust, as meaning something very soft and tender, without much caring what: but with this general activity of intellect came a necessity for even poets to appear to know something of what they professed to talk of. Thomson and Cowper looked at the trees and hills which so many ingenious gentlemen had rhymed about so long without looking at them at all, and the effect of the operation on poetry was like the discovery of a new world. Painting shared the influence, and the principles of picturesque beauty were explored by adventurous essayists with indefatigable pertinacity. The success which attended these experiments, and the pleasure which resulted from them, had the usual effect of all new enthusiasms, that of turning the heads of a few unfortunate persons, the patriarchs of the age of brass, who, mistaking the prominent novelty for the all-important totality, seem to have ratiocinated much in the following manner: 'Poetical genius is the finest of all things, and we feel that we have more of it than any one ever had. The way to bring it to perfection is to cultivate poetical impressions exclusively. Poetical impressions can be received only among natural scenes: for all that is artificial is anti-poetical. Society is artificial, therefore we will live out of society. The mountains are natural, therefore we will live in the mountains. There we shall be shining models of purity and virtue, passing the whole day in the innocent and amiable occupation of going up and down hill, receiving poetical impressions, and communicating them in immortal verse to admiring generations.' To some such perversion of intellect we owe that egregious confraternity of rhymesters, known by the name of the Lake Poets; who certainly did receive and communicate to the world some of the most extraordinary poetical impressions that ever were heard of, and ripened into models of public virtue, too splendid to need illustration. They wrote verses on a new principle; saw rocks and rivers in a new light; and remaining studiously ignorant of history, society, and human nature, cultivated the phantasy only at the expense of the memory and the reason; and contrived, though they had retreated from the world for the express purpose of seeing nature as she was, to see her only as she was not, converting the land they lived in into a sort of fairy-land, which they peopled with mysticisms and chimæras. This gave what is called a new tone to poetry, and conjured up a herd of desperate imitators, who have brought the age of brass prematurely to its dotage.

The descriptive poetry of the present day has been called by its cultivators a return to nature. Nothing is more impertinent than this pretension. Poetry cannot travel out of the regions of its birth, the uncultivated lands of semi-civilized men. Mr Wordsworth, the great leader of the returners to nature, cannot describe a scene under his own eyes without putting into it the shadow of a Danish boy or the living ghost of Lucy Gray, or some similar phantastical parturition of the moods of his own mind.

In the origin and perfection of poetry, all the associations of life were composed of poetical materials. With us it is decidedly the reverse. We know too that there are no Dryads in Hyde-park nor Naiads in the Regent's canal. But barbaric manners and supernatural interventions are essential to poetry. Either in the scene, or in the time, or in both, it must be remote from our ordinary perceptions. While the historian and the philosopher are advancing in, and accelerating, the progress of knowledge, the poet is wallowing in the rubbish of departed ignorance, and raking up the ashes of dead savages to find gewgaws and rattles for the grown babies of the age. Mr Scott digs up the poachers and cattle-stealers of the ancient border. Lord Byron cruises for thieves and pirates on the shores of the Morea and among the Greek islands. Mr Southey wades through ponderous volumes of travels and old chronicles, from which he carefully selects all that is false, useless, and absurd, as being essentially poetical; and when he has a commonplace book full of monstrosities, strings them into an epic. Mr Wordsworth picks up village legends from old women and sextons; and Mr Coleridge, to the valuable information acquired from similar sources, superadds the dreams of crazy theologians and the mysticisms of German metaphysics, and favours the world with visions in verse, in which the quadruple elements of sexton, old woman, Jeremy Taylor, and Emanuel Kant, are harmonized into a delicious poetical compound. Mr Moore presents us with a Persian, and Mr Campbell with a Pennsylvanian tale, both formed on the same principle as Mr Southey's epics, by extracting from a perfunctory and desultory perusal of a collection of voyages and travels, all that useful investigation would not seek for and that common sense would reject.

These disjointed relics of tradition and fragments of second hand observation, being woven into a tissue of verse, constructed on what Mr Coleridge calls a new principle (that is, no principle at all), compose a modern-antique compound of frippery and barbarism, in which the puling sentimentality of the present time is grafted on the misrepresented ruggedness of the past into a heterogeneous congeries of unamalgamating manners, sufficient to impose on the common readers of poetry, over whose understandings the poet of this class possesses that commanding advantage, which, in all circumstances and conditions of life, a man who knows something, however little, always possesses over one who knows nothing.

A poet in our times is a semi-barbarian in a civilized community. He lives in the days that are past. His ideas, thoughts, feelings, associations, are all with barbarous manners, obsolete customs, and exploded superstitions. The march of his intellect is like that of a crab, backward. The brighter the light diffused around him by the progress of reason, the thicker is the darkness of antiquated barbarism, in which he buries himself like a mole, to throw up the barren hillocks of his Cimmerian labours. The philosophic mental tranquillity which looks round with an equal eye on all external things, collects a store of ideas, discriminates their relative value, assigns to all their proper place, and from the materials of useful knowledge thus collected, appreciated, and arranged, forms new combinations that impress the stamp of their power and utility on the real business of life, is diametrically the reverse of that frame of mind which poetry inspires, or from which poetry can emanate. The highest inspirations of poetry are resolvable into three ingredients: the rant of unregulated passion, the whine of exaggerated feeling, and the cant of factitious sentiment: and can therefore serve

6

only to ripen a splendid lunatic like Alexander, a puling driveller like Werter, or a morbid dreamer like Wordsworth. It can never make a philosopher, nor a statesman, nor in any class of life a useful or rational man. It cannot claim the slightest share in any one of the comforts and utilities of life of which we have witnessed so many and so rapid advances. But though not useful, it may be said it is highly ornamental, and deserves to be cultivated for the pleasure it yields. Even if this be granted, it does not follow that a writer of poetry in the present state of society is not a waster of his own time, and a robber of that of others. Poetry is not one of these arts which, like painting, require repetition and multiplication, in order to be diffused among society. There are more good poems already existing than are sufficient to employ that portion of life which any mere reader and recipient of poetical impressions should devote to them, and these having been produced in poetical times, are far superior in all the characteristics of poetry to the artificial reconstructions of a few morbid ascetics in unpoetical times. To read the promiscuous rubbish of the present time to the exclusion of the select treasures of the past, is to substitute the worse for the better variety of the same mode of enjoyment.

But in whatever degree poetry is cultivated, it must necessarily be to the neglect of some branch of useful study: and it is a lamentable spectacle to see minds, capable of better things, running to seed in the specious indolence of these empty aimless mockeries of intellectual exertion. Poetry was the mental rattle that awakened the attention of intellect in the infancy of civil society: but for the maturity of mind to make a serious business of the playthings of its childhood, is as absurd as for a full-grown man to rub his gums with coral, and cry to be charmed to sleep by the jingle of silver bells.

As to that small portion of our contemporary poetry, which is neither descriptive, nor narrative, nor dramatic, and which, for want of a better name, may be called ethical, the most distinguished portion of it, consisting merely of querulous egotistical rhapsodies, to express the writer's high dissatisfaction with the world and everything in it, serves only to confirm what has been said of the semi-barbarous character of poets, who from singing dithyrambics and 'Io Triumphe', while society was savage, grow rabid, and out of their element, as it becomes polished and enlightened.

Now, when we consider that it is not to the thinking and studious, and scientific and philosophical part of the community, not to those whose minds are bent on the pursuit and promotion of permanently useful ends and aims, that poets must address their minstrelsy, but to that much larger portion of the reading public, whose minds are not awakened to the desire of valuable knowledge, and who are indifferent to any thing beyond being charmed, moved, excited, affected, and exalted: charmed by harmony, moved by sentiment, excited by passion, affected by pathos, and exalted by sublimity: harmony, which is language on the rack of Procrustes; sentiment, which is canting egotism in the mask of refined feeling; passion, which is the commotion of a weak and selfish mind; pathos, which is the whining of an unmanly spirit; and sublimity, which is the inflation of an empty head: when we consider that the great and permanent interests of human society become more and more the main spring of intellectual pursuit; that in proportion as they become so, the sub-ordinacy of the ornamental to the useful will be more and more seen and acknowledged; and that therefore the progress of useful art and science, and of moral and political knowledge, will continue more and more to withdraw attention from frivolous and unconducive, to solid and conducive studies: that therefore the poetical audience will not only continually diminish in the proportion of its number to that of the rest of the reading public, but will also sink lower and lower in the comparison of intellectual acquirement: when we consider that the poet must still please his audience, and must therefore continue to sink to their level, while the rest of the community is rising above it: we may easily conceive that the day is not distant, when the degraded state of every species of poetry will be as generally recognized as that of dramatic poetry has long been: and this not from any decrease either of intellectual power, or intellectual acquisition, but because intellectual power and intellectual acquisition have turned themselves into other and better channels, and have abandoned the cultivation and the fate of poetry to the degenerate fry of modern rhymesters, and their olympic judges, the magazine critics, who continue to debate and promulgate oracles about poetry, as if it were still what it was in the Homeric age, the all-in-all of intellectual progression, and as if there were no such things in existence as mathematicians, astronomers, chemists, moralists, metaphysicians, historians, politicians, and political economists, who have built into the upper air of intelligence a pyramid, from the summit of which they see the modern Parnassus far beneath them, and, knowing how small a place it occupies in the comprehensiveness of their prospect, smile at the little ambition and the circumscribed perceptions with which the drivellers and mountebanks upon it are contending for the poetical palm and the critical chair.

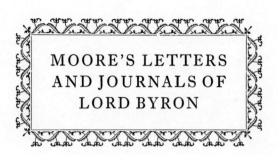

MOORE'S LETTERS
AND JOURNALS OF
LORD BYRON

MOORE'S LETTERS AND JOURNALS
OF LORD BYRON*

THIS first volume takes us at some disadvantage. *Respice finem* is especially applicable to biography. Much of the pleasure, as well as of the utility, arising from works of this description, consists in the study of character: and in this point of view, the last act of the drama of life often throws light on the first. Few men are so ingenuous as to enable their most intimate friends to discriminate very accurately the artificial from the real in their characters: we mean by the artificial, the assumed semblance, which, on an adequate occasion, would be thrown aside as easily as a mask and domino, as easily as the character of priest was thrown aside in the French Revolution by many of the dignified persons to whom it ceased to bring revenue. Extreme cases of this artificial character are to be found in the stolidity of the elder Brutus, in the madness of Edgar, and the folly of Leon. In a minor degree, this assumption of an unreal exterior exists more or less in all men: few have been so fortunate in this world's transactions, as never to see an old friend with a new face: it is time alone, (ὁ παντέλεγχος χρόνος, as Sophocles most happily says,) that shews whether the young popularity-carping senator, is a true Patriot, or a Whig, acting patriotism; whether the young soldier of a republic is, at heart, a Napoleon or a Washington. By the real in character, we mean those qualities, moral and intellectual, which remain unchanged through the entire course of

---

* *Letters and Journals of Lord Byron, with Notices of his Life.* By Thomas Moore. 2 vols, 4to. Vol. I. London, 1830 (Murray).

'man's maturer years'; and which the collision of events, however adverse, only serves to develop and confirm. For examples
of these qualities in their worst and best forms, we need look no
further than, on the one hand, to the love of excitement in
gamblers and drunkards, whom it conducts to ruin and the
grave: and on the other, to the love of country and mankind in
the characters of Washington, Jefferson, Franklin, and their
principal coadjutors in the North American Revolution.

Solon bade Crœsus look to the end of life, before he could
pronounce on individual happiness: it is not less necessary to do
so before pronouncing a final judgment on individual character.
The principal attraction of this work is the light which it has
been expected to throw on the character of Lord Byron. So
far, it has, to us at least, thrown little new light upon it, and
much of that little by no means calculated to render any
essential service to his memory.

Lord Byron was always 'himself the great sublime he drew'.
Whatever figures filled up the middle and back ground of his
pictures, the fore-ground was invariably consecrated to his own.
As somebody, on a different occasion, said of Mr Coleridge, 'he
made the public his confidant': but his confidences were only
half-confidences, more calculated to stimulate than to satisfy
curiosity. He gave full vent to his feelings: but he hinted, rather
than communicated, the circumstances of their origin: and he
mixed up in his hints shadowy self-accusations of imaginary
crimes, on which, of course, the liberal public put the worst
possible construction. Indeed, both in his writings and conversation he dealt, in his latter years especially, very largely in
mystification; and said many things which have brought his
faithful reminiscents into scrapes, by making them report, what
others, knowing he could not have believed, think he never
could have asserted: which are very different matters. His confidences to Captain Medwin and Mr Leigh Hunt, were many
of them of this mystificatory class. They were of that sort of
confidences which are usually reposed in the butt of an Italian
opera buffa; where the words *'in confidenza'* invariably signify,

that there is not a word of truth in any thing the party is going to say. Lord Byron was early distinguished by a scrupulous regard to truth: but the attrition of the world blunts the fine edge of veracity, even in the most ingenuous dispositions: and making the most liberal allowance for misapprehension and misrepresentation, we still think it impossible to read Medwin's and Hunt's reminiscences, without perceiving that those two worthy gentlemen had been very egregiously *mystified*. Lord Byron talked to them in the same spirit in which he wrote much of his *badinage* in Don Juan: such for instance as the passage:

> I've bribed my grandmother's review, the British.
> I sent it in a letter to the editor,
> Who thanked me duly by return of post:
> I'm for a handsome article his creditor, &c.

The editor took this as a serious charge, and most pathetically implored Lord Byron, as a gentleman and a man of honour, to disavow it. He was handsomely laughed at for his pains: for nobody believed the charge, or regarded it as having been seriously made.

Mr Moore bears testimony to Lord Byron's disposition in this way. He says of a letter to Mr Dallas:

> In addition to the temptation, never easily resisted by him, of displaying his wit at the expense of his character, he was here addressing a person who, though, no doubt, well-meaning, was evidently one of those officious, self-satisfied advisers, whom it was the delight of Lord Byron at all times to astonish and *mystify*. The tricks which, when a boy, he played upon the Nottingham quack, Lavender, were but the first of a long series with which, through life, he amused himself, at the expense of all the numerous quacks, whom his celebrity and sociability drew around him (p. 135).

It must be evident that a person, who would write in this vein, would also talk in it, especially to persons whom he did not much respect. We shall not enter into the casuistry of the question, nor endeavour to decide how far this same weapon of

mystification may be justifiably employed, either for the purpose of playing with self-conceited credulity, or for that of
parrying or misleading impertinent curiosity. Great men have
used it, and great men have justified it:

> Quantunque il simular sia le più volte
> Ripreso, e dia di mala mente indici,
> Si trova pur' in molte cose e molte
> Aver fatti evidenti benefici,
> E danni, e biasmi, e morti aver già tolte,
> Che non conversiam sempre con gli amici,
> In questa, assai piu oscura, che serena,
> Vita mortal, tutta d'invidia piena.*

For ourselves, we hope we shall never adopt, we certainly
shall not justify, the practice. We are for the maxim of the old
British bards: 'The Truth against the World.' But if there be
any one case of human life, in which this practice is justifiable,
it is in the case of an individual living out of society, and much
talked of in it, and haunted in his retirement by varieties of the
small Boswell or eavesdropping genus, who, as a very little penetration must shew him, would take the first opportunity of selling his confidences to the public, if he should happen to drop
any thing for which the prurient appetite of the reading rabble
would present a profitable market. Some light will be thrown
on this point by Mr Hunt's naïve observation, that the 'natural
Byron' was never seen but when he was half-tipsy, and that the
said Byron was particularly careful not to get tipsy in Mr Hunt's
company. The 'artificial Byron' was all mockery and despair;
and allowed himself to be regularly set down, half a dozen times
a day, by the repartees of Mr Hunt, and Mrs Hunt, and all the
little Master Hunts. In short,

> Man but a rush against Othello's breast,
> And he retired.†

---

* Ariosto: Canto IV.
† The following extracts from Mr Hunt's publication will substantiate
what we have said in the text. [These extracts, totalling nearly 200
lines, are here omitted — Ed.]

We did not review Mr Hunt's publication. The Quarterly Review did it ample justice; and though that Review left unsaid some things which we should have said, and said some things which we certainly should not have said, it would have been *actum agere* to go again over the same ground. We are not solicitous about the motives which influenced the Quarterly Reviewers. They had an old political enemy at a manifest moral disadvantage. The querulous egotisms, the scaturient vanity bubbling up in every page like the hundred fountains of the river Hoangho, the readiness to violate all the confidences of private life, the intrinsic nothingness of what the writer had it in his power to tell, the shallow mockeries of philosophical thinking, the quaint and silly figures of speech, the out-of-the-way notions of morals and manners, the eternal reference of every thing to self, the manifest labour and effort to inflate a mass of insignificancies into the bulk of a quarto, for the sake of the liberal bookseller, who wanted to append a given number of pages to the name of Lord Byron, the constantly recurring 'Io Triumphe' over the excellent hits and clinches of the author and his family, and the obvious *malus animus* of the entire work; presented so many inviting prominences to the hand of castigation, that the Quarterly could for once come forth on fair ground, and flagellate an opponent without having recourse to its old art of wilful misrepresentation.

Many traces of that spirit of *badinage* which says things not meant or expected to be believed, and which literal interpretation would turn into something never dreamed of by the writer, occur throughout the letters in this volume. For example, Lord Byron writing from Constantinople, says to his mother:

> H. who will deliver this is bound straight for England: and as he is bursting with his travels, I shall not anticipate his narratives, but merely beg you not to believe one word he says, but reserve your ear for me, if you have any desire to be acquainted with the truth.

No one, who reads this volume, will suppose this to be anything but jest; but we can easily conceive his reminiscents reporting it thus: 'He had a very bad opinion of Mr Hobhouse's veracity, and emphatically cautioned me against believing a word he said'.

We shall not multiply instances. The volume abounds with them. We believe that Captain Medwin and Mr Leigh Hunt were both gentlemen to take every thing literally. Lord Byron did not, in truth, admit either of them into his confidence, more than one step further, if even that, than he did the public in general: and their imperfect and flippant communications answered scarcely any purpose but to disappoint expectation.

Curiosity was never more strongly excited, nor disappointment more strongly experienced, than by the memoirs which Lord Byron left of himself, and which Mr Moore committed to the flames. Mr Moore calls them 'the memoirs or rather memoranda, which it was thought expedient, for various reasons, to sacrifice'. (p. 655) These being gone beyond recovery, Mr Moore remained, with the reputation of being the best-informed person in the kingdom on the subject of the noble poet, of having access to the most ample materials for his biography, and of being the best qualified person to put those materials together.

It turns out, however, most unluckily, that all that is best worth telling is not fit to be told. In the points about which the public were most curious, what was before mystery, is still mystery. It remains, like Bottom's dream, in the repositories of the incommunicable.

> *Bottom.* The eye of man hath not heard; the ear of man hath not seen; man's hand is not able to taste, his tongue to conceive, nor his heart to report, what my dream was.
>
> Masters, I am to discourse wonders: but ask me not what; for if I tell you, I am no true Athenian. I will tell you every thing, right as it fell out.
>
> *Quince.* Let us hear, sweet Bottom.
>
> *Bottom.* Not a word of me. All that I will tell you is, that the duke hath dined.

And of matter about as important as the duke's dinner is at least one half of this goodly volume composed.

We shall now give an account of this first volume, making such remarks as suggest themselves, and reserving our general observations till the conclusion of the second.

The work begins with an account of Lord Byron's ancestry. 'In the character of the noble poet,' says Mr Moore, 'the pride of ancestry was undoubtedly one of the most decided features.' His descent is cursorily traced from 'Ralph de Burun, whose name ranks high in Dooms-day book, among the tenants of land in Nottinghamshire', (page 1) through Sir John Byron the Little, with the Great Beard (page 3) who, 'at the dissolution of the monasteries, obtained, by a royal grant, the church and priory of Newstead, with the lands adjoining': Sir John Byron, who, in the year 1643, was created by Charles the 1st 'Baron Byron of Rochdale in the county of Lancaster', and is described as having been to the last a most faithful, persevering, and dis- interested follower of the king: down to the grandfather, grand uncle and father of the poet: the first Mr, afterwards Admiral Byron, whose shipwreck and sufferings, about the year 1750, awakened, in no small degree, the attention and sympathy of the public: the second, the Lord Byron, who, in the year 1765, stood his trial before the House of Peers for killing in a duel, or rather scuffle, his relation and neighbour, Mr Chaworth: and the third, Captain Byron, a worthless profligate, who married, first, the divorced wife of Lord Carmarthen, whom he had pre- viously carried off from her husband; and afterwards, on her death, Miss Catharine Gordon, only child and heiress of George Gordon, esq. of Gight. The only offspring of the first marriage was the honourable Augusta Byron, now the wife of Colonel Leigh: the only offspring of the second was the subject of this memoir, who was born in Holles Street, London, on the 22nd of January 1788: by which time his mother, who had been married in 1785, was reduced from competence to a pittance of 150*l.* per annum; her husband having squandered the whole of her fortune. The lady was no exception to Master Silence's axiom, that 'women are shrews, both short and tall': on the contrary, she was a virago of the first magnitude. This hopeful pair separated in 1790; and the husband died in 1791. Little Byron was left with his mother, who taught him to rage and storm; and his nurse, who taught him to repeat the psalms, and sang him to sleep with stories and legends. He read the Bible through and through, before he was eight years old. The Old Testament he read as a pleasure, the New as a task.

The malformation of his foot, occasioned by an accident at his birth, was a subject of pain, inconvenience, and mortification to him, from his earliest years.

He began his scholastic education at a cheap day-school in Aberdeen, where he made little progress. In 1796 he was removed by his mother, for the change of air, into the Highlands, where he acquired his first enthusiasm for mountain scenery: and fell in love at eight years old with a 'Highland Mary' of his own. On these two points, mountain scenery and precocious love, Mr Moore philosophizes.

In 1798, by the death of his grand uncle, he succeeded to the title and estates, the latter being much involved, and the former, consequently, a great calamity. He was now placed in the hands of a quack, at Nottingham, named Lavender, who tortured him grievously under pretence of curing his foot, and, during this infliction, he received lessons in Latin from a respectable schoolmaster, Mr Rogers.

In 1799, he was removed to London, and placed under the medical care of Dr Baillie, and in the scholastic establishment of Dr Glennie at Dulwich, where, having been carefully untaught the little he had learned in Scotland, he started afresh and began to make way: but was much impeded by his mother having him too much at home.

In 1800, he had a second boyish passion for his young cousin Miss Parker.

In 1801, he went to Harrow, 'as little prepared', says Dr Glennie, 'as it is natural to suppose from two years of elementary instruction, thwarted by every art that could estrange the mind of youth from preceptor, from school, and from all serious study'.

At Harrow, however, he distinguished himself as an athlete, neglecting his school-books, and picked up some general knowledge by reading history, philosophy, and so forth, contrary to the good order and discipline of our public establishments for eradicating the love of letters. He fought his way into the respect of his school-fellows. A vast deal of childish matter is here narrated, very inficete and unprofitable to peruse.

In 1803, he fell in love with his cousin, Miss Chaworth. As much is supposed to hang upon this unsuccessful attachment, and as the narration will serve as a favourable specimen of the matter and manner of the work, we shall extract the entire passage, in which this event is related: [A quotation of seven pages follows.]

* * *

Now that this affair gave a colour to all his future life, we do not in the slightest degree believe. It was his own mind that gave the colour to the affair. It was his disposition to aim always at unattainable things. If he had married this idol, he would very soon have drawn the same conclusion respecting her, which he drew respecting all the objects of his more successful pursuit:

> 'Tis an old lesson; Time approves it true,
> And they who know it best deplore it most;
> When all is won that all desire to woo,
> The paltry prize is hardly worth the cost.
>> *Childe Harold:* Canto I., St. 35.

Through life he aimed at what he could not compass. He took the best substitutes which circumstances placed in his way, and consoled himself with a handmaid for the loss of a Helen: the latter being still longed for because she was inaccessible. As a Greek poet says,

> "Ἀ'γ ὕς τὰν βάλανον τὰν μὲν ἔχει, τὰν δ' ἔραται
>   λαβεῖν,
> Κἀγὼ παῖδα καλὴν τὰν μὲν ἔχω, τὰν δ' ἔραμαι
>   λαβεῖν.

There is nothing singular in this state of mind, nor even in a man's deluding himself into the belief, that a single disappointment of this sort has coloured his life. The singularity is, finding another man to believe it.

Apropos of Lord Byron's reading at Harrow, Mr Moore has a side cut or two at classical literature (pp. 59, 60) which, when we remember his Epicurean, and certain observations thereon,* makes us think of the fox and the grapes.

In 1805, Lord Byron was removed to Trinity College, Cambridge. In 1806, being on a visit to his mother at Southwell, the lady's temper exploded on some occasion, and she converted the poker and tongs into the thunderbolts of her wrath. From this Juno Tonans and her missiles he fled to London, and made it his chief care to keep himself out of her reach.

In 1807, he printed a small volume of poems, for private distribution among his friends. This being a very interesting subject, and very safe to dilate upon, occupies a large share of the biographer's attention. There is a good deal also about his enjoyment of athletic exercises, his ignorance of horses, his fondness for dogs and fire-arms, his belief in second-sight, *fetches*, and so forth; his horror of growing fat, his sensitiveness on the score of his foot, his multifarious reading, and the delight with which he seasoned his academical studies by a copy of Mother Goose's Tales, which he bought of a hawker. *Res memoranda novis annalibus.*

A long list is given of the books which he had read up to that time, November 1807. It is very copious, especially in history. Few young men at College, Mr Moore thinks, had read so much: we think so too: we may make large deductions from it, and still think so. There is, however, a way of scouting through books, which some people call reading, and we are afraid much of the reading here set down was of that description. 'Greek and Latin poets, without number.' We are sceptical on this point at any rate. If he had read and understood—we include

* *Westminster Review*, No. XVI.

understanding in our idea of reading—if he had read and understood as many Greek poets as he could count on his fingers, he never could have fallen into the preposterous blunder which he committed in Don Juan:

> The European with the Asian shore
> Sprinkled with palaces; the *ocean stream*
> Here and there studded with a seventy four, &c.
>
> Canto V., St. 3.

He says in a note on '*the ocean stream*':

> This expression of Homer has been much criticised. It hardly answers to our Atlantic ideas of the ocean, but is sufficiently applicable to the Hellespont and the Bosphorus, with the Aegean intersected with islands.

Who were the parties that had criticized Homer out of his obvious meaning, we know not: but could it have been necessary to tell a man who had 'read Greek poets without number', that, according to the ideas of the ancients, the Ocean River flowed entirely round the earth, and that the seas were inlets from it? The Shield of Achilles alone would have set this point at rest, without looking to any more recondite sources. The River Ocean surrounded the work immediately within the edge of the shield; and the earth, which it enclosed, was imaged in the interior.

> Ἐν δὲ τίθει ποταμοῖο μέγα σθένος Ὠκενοῖο,
> Ἄντυγα πὰρ πυμάτην σάκεος πύκα ποιητοῖο.
>
> 'Hic utique manifestum fit,' says Heyne, 'auctorem voluisse orbem terrarum in clypeo esse adumbratum.'

'Much criticized' indeed! It is impossible that the expression could ever have been criticized at all, except by mere English readers, puzzling themselves over Pope's translation, or Milton's passage about Leviathan. But let those who wish to see the matter in broad daylight, read the beginning of the Periegesis of Dionysius.

Ex pede Herculem. A man who could speculate in this strain, after reading Greek and Latin poets without number (unhappily they are too easily numerable) must have read to little good purpose. 'The utility of reading', says Horne Tooke, 'depends not on the swallow, but on the digestion.'

Lord Byron had read enough to produce a general effect with a multitude of inaccurate recollections. This is the best sort of reading for those who aim merely at amusing the public: and for the space of his life before us, he aimed at nothing higher.

> 'I see', he says (October 1810), 'the Lady of the Lake advertised. Of course, it is in his old ballad style, and pretty. After all, Scott is the best of them. The end of all scribblement is to amuse, and he certainly succeeds there.' (p. 241)

And in the same spirit, Captain Medwin reports him to have said: 'The great object is effect, no matter how produced.' His a reading, and that of his friend and biographer, are much of piece in this respect, and remind us of a French treatise on music, which we saw advertised the other day, as containing *tout ce qui est nécessaire pour en parler sans l'avoir étudié*.

His life, at college, was not different from that of most young gentlemen there.

> 'Since my last,' he says (writing from Trinity College, Cambridge, July 5, 1807) 'I have determined to reside another year at Granta, as my rooms, &c., &c. are finished in great style, several old friends come up again, and many new acquaintances made, consequently my inclination leads me forward; and I shall return to college in October, if still alive. My life here has been one continued routine of dissipation—out at different places every day, engaged to more dinners, &c., &c. than my *stay* would permit me to fulfil. At this moment, I write with a bottle of claret in my *head*, and *tears* in my *eyes,* for I have just parted with my Cornelian, who spent the evening with me.' (p. 113)

Farther on, he says more seriously (Jan. 21, 1808):

> I am a member of the University of Cambridge, where I shall take my degree of A.M. this term: but were reasoning, eloquence, or virtue, the objects of my search, Granta is not their metropolis,

nor is the place of her situation an El Dorado, far less an Utopia. The intellects of her children are as stagnant as her Cam, and their pursuits limited to the church, not of Christ, but of the nearest benefice. (p. 134)

Mr Moore philosophizes on this passage, and is of opinion that the hatred and contempt which Milton and Gray entertained for Cambridge, and Gibbon and Locke for Oxford, 'may well be thought to have had their origin in that antipathy to the trammels of discipline which is not unusually observable among the characteristics of genius'; and goes on discussing 'the tendency of genius and taste to rebel against discipline',

> In proper terms, such as men smatter,
> When they throw out, and miss the matter:

And here Mr Moore misses the matter most completely, as, in all cases in which a grain of philosophy is requisite, he makes a point of doing. If the Universities can make nothing of genius, their discipline, if it were good for anything, might make something of mediocrity or of dullness: but their discipline is mere pretence, and is limited to the non-essentials of education: they settle down mediocrity into a quiet hatred of literature, and confirm a questionable dunce into a hopeless, incurable, and self-satisfied blockhead. Milton, Locke, Gibbon, and Gray (and Lord Byron himself), all professedly learned a great deal in spite of all the efforts of their respective universities to prevent them, and when our most illustrious names in poetry, philosophy, and history, are arrayed against the universities, it is, forsooth, according to Mr Moore, the dislike of genius to discipline, and not the antipathy of intellect, knowledge, reason and truth, to ignorance, avarice, and political servility, in the false assumption of learning and science.

We shall not, however, leave this question to inference. We shall show in their own words, *why* Milton, Gibbon, and Gray hated and despised their respective universities. [Six pages of quotations follow.]

*   *   *

It is really something *un peu fort*, even for Mr Moore, to pretend that these learned and laborious men, all of whom subjected their minds to the severest discipline, disliked their universities only because discipline is distasteful to genius. But the universities are influential, and Mr Moore must stand well with the influential in all its forms. This will be more and more apparent as we proceed.

In 1807, Lord Byron published his 'Hours of Idleness', and in 1808, the Edinburgh Review attacked it in the spirit of its usual dealings with all authors, young authors especially, who were not within the corrupt circle of its political and literary favouritism, Mr Moore had been similarly dealt with not long previously: but both Mr Moore and Lord Byron successively forced themselves into the enchanted circle: the first having introduced himself by proposing to shoot his critic, which proved that he was not only a gentleman but a great poet: the second by laying about him, with the figurative horse-whip of satire, indiscriminately on his reviewer, and on all he had ever praised, which, as the public sided with the young satirist, set his pretensions to genius in an entirely new light. The review having been written without principle, and merely as a piece of catering for idle malignity, 'the most gifted of critics' pocketed the invective which consigned him to the Tolbooth, and the three 'gifted' parties, of whom one had challenged two, and two had, in critical phraseology, cut up two, (Moore having challenged Jeffrey and Byron, Jeffrey having cut up Moore and Byron, and Byron having cut up Jeffrey and Moore), became three of the best friends in this literary world, to the great advantage of their respective reputations with the enlightened and discerning public. As Mr Moore is both poet and musician, we recommend this to him as a matchless subject for a catch.

Mr Moore apologizes, in a very lame and irresolute way, for his friend the critic's original treatment of his friend the poet. 'The knave, sir, is mine honest friend', says Davy to Justice Shallow, pleading for Vizor of Wincot. We shall pass over this point for the present, because we shall have a better opportunity of noticing the system which the Edinburgh Review adopted in its literary criticisms.

Much information is given respecting the progress of the Satire through the press. Lord Byron's sole standard of judgment of persons was in his own personal feelings of favour and resentment. Mr Moore euphonizes this into 'the susceptibility of new impressions and influences which rendered both his judgment and feelings so variable'. It is amusing to see how Lord Carlisle was turned from a Roscommon into a blockhead; Professor Smith, the English Lyrist, from one who discredited even the University, to one who almost redeemed his name: Sir William Gell, from coxcomb to classic, by a single stroke of the pen, because, in his chrysalis state between coxcomb and classic, Lord Byron accidentally became acquainted with him; and so forth. This was pretty much the way in which he formed his opinions through life.

* * *

In 1811 he lost his mother and his two friends, Wingfield and Charles Skinner Matthews. Mr Moore gives some account of this latter gentleman, who, it seems, like his noble friend, had 'lost his way in the mazes of scepticism'. This infection, labyrinth, canker, blastment, light that leads astray, cloud, eclipse, &c., &c., &c. so bewilders Mr Moore with its mere imagination, that he loses his own way irretrievably in a labyrinth of figures. We cannot help him out of it: but requesting him, as Falstaff did Pistol, to deliver himself like a man of this world, we will make a remark or two on the subject that has made 'chaos come again' amongst his metaphors.

We find, in the letters of Lord Byron to Mr Dallas, Mr Hodgson, and Mr Gifford, replies to expostulations and arguments which those gentlemen had addressed to him on the subject of his infidelity. Now, if any of these gentlemen, after his death, had lamented his infidelity in writing of him to the public, it would have been consistent with their conduct towards him during his life. But in his letters to Mr Moore, and in all

Mr Moore's account of their intercourse, there is not a vestige of any expostulation or argument on the subject addressed to him by Mr Moore. He therefore comes forward now with a very ill grace, saying that of Lord Byron, after his death, which there is no evidence to shew, and not the least reason to believe, he ever said to him during his life. We think it quite of a piece with Mr Moore's general system of acquiescence with the influential in all its forms, to conclude, that having first courted the favour of Lord Byron by silence, at least, on the one hand, he now courts that of the public by talk on the other.

'The staple commodity of the present age in England,' says Lord Byron himself somewhere, 'is cant: cant moral, cant religious, cant political; but always cant.' How much of this staple commodity there may be in Mr Moore's lamentations, we shall leave our readers to judge.

Lord Byron's letters to Mr Moore contain not a syllable of replication to any shadow of an expressed solicitude on the subject of his infidelity. It was assuredly very unkind in Mr Moore not even to offer his hand to extricate him from 'the labyrinth in which he was bewildered'; 'the eclipse in which he was labouring'; more especially as, from the confidence with which Mr Moore ascribes error to Lord Byron, he must be himself in the possession of something very nearly approaching the infallibility of the Catholic church. A man cannot say unhesitatingly, that another is grossly wrong, unless in the confidence that he himself is perfectly right. We think it, therefore, a very unfriendly measure on his part to have withheld his 'short and easy method' from his deistical friend, while he was yet living and able to profit by it; and now to come forward, shaking his head over him, and pelting his infidel memory with a hailstorm of metaphors, by way of making a good orthodox presentment of himself in the eyes of the religious community. But we do not think that any direct-dealing man, be his religious opinions what they may, can admire the figure which Mr Moore makes on this occasion.

In all his remarks on this subject, it is most manifest to us that he has no other aim than to say fine and palatable things. To the latter quality let those who relish them speak. To the former we will say a word or two.

'The canker showed itself in the morn and dew of youth.' What is a canker in the morn, or a canker in the dew? He means, we presume, a canker on the rosebud while the morning dew is upon it. Does the canker-worm begin its operations by showing itself? Does it come with the morning dew? Neither. There is a false metaphor to start with. 'The canker showed itself in the morn and dew of youth', when the effect of such 'blastments';— here the canker-worm is turned into a 'blastment', a blastment coming with morning dew: let Mr Moore watch his garden twelve months round, and if he find blight or blastment of any description coming with morning dew, let him publish the particulars of what will really be a great phytological and meteorological discover. Thus is the false metaphor doubly falsified. 'When the effect of such blastments is for every reason most fatal, and, in addition to the real misfortune of being an unbeliever at any age, he exhibited the rare and melancholy spectacle of an unbelieving school-boy. The same prematurity of development, which brought his passions and genius so early into action, enabled him also to anticipate this worst, dreariest result of reason.' We have suddenly lost sight of the canker-worm, and now we find that, according to Mr Moore, error is a result of reason. This is a discovery in logic, worthy of his preceding discoveries in physics.

A little after this we find that 'Lord Byron had begun to bewilder himself in the mazes of scepticism', that is, in other words, had set about leading himself astray: a somewhat Irish process: 'his mind disported itself most wantonly on the brink of all that is most solemn and awful'; here he is out of the laby-rinth and on the edge of a precipice: but 'he never was at any time of his life a confirmed unbeliever'. Why, then, what was he? Mr Moore does not know. If he was not a confirmed unbeliever, he was to a certain extent a believer; and then the question arises, to what extent? and whether among all the sects into which the Christian world is divided, there was not one which would have received him within its pale?

'Infidelity,' says a wiser man than Mr Moore [Richard Payne Knight, in the preface to the *Progress of Civil Society*, p. xvii], 'is a vague term of general accusation, which every hypocrite or fanatic applies to those who appear to be less hypocritical or fanatical than himself. I shall, therefore, take no further notice of it than merely to say, that I have never printed or written any opinion on the subject of Christianity, which I cannot prove to be consistent with the duties of a good subject, a good citizen, and a good man: I might perhaps add, of a good Christian, did I understand the meaning of the term, or know the duties which it implies; but having found, by some little reading and observation, that it has not only had a different signification in every age and country, but in the mouth of almost every individual who has ever used it, I will not pretend to it, till its meaning is so far determined, that I may know whether I can justly pretend to it or not. What is established by law, I respect and obey; but still, as it appears to me to be in many respects extremely different from what was in-culcated by the Founder of Christianity and his immediate suc-cessors, I am not certain that I can thereby claim the title of a good Christian.'

Mr Moore wishes to persuade the public that he denies the right of private judgment in respect of religious belief. He seems to think that belief can be enforced, and treats disbelief as an offence. He talks of infidelity as 'a dangerous state of freedom from moral responsibility'. We will cite for his instruction, a passage from the writings of one of the most sober-minded, calm-judging men, and one of the greatest benefactors of his species, that the modern world had produced: a religious man too himself, Thomas Jefferson.

On the subject of religion, Jefferson writes to his young friend Peter Carr:

Your reason is now mature enough to examine this object. In the first place, divest yourself of all bias in favour of novelty and singularity of opinion. Indulge them in any other subject rather than that of religion. It is too important, and the consequences of error may be too serious. On the other hand, shake off all the fears and servile prejudices, under which weak minds are servilely crouched. Fix reason firmly in her seat, and call to her tribunal every fact, every opinion. Question with boldness even the existence of a God; because if there be one, he must more approve the homage of reason, than of blindfolded fear. You will naturally examine, first, the religion of your own country.

* * *

Do not be frightened from this inquiry by any fear of its consequences. If it ends in a belief that there is no God, you will find incitements to virtue in the comfort and pleasantness you feel in its exercise, and the love of others which it will procure you. If you find reason to believe there is a God, a consciousness that you are acting under his eye, and that he approves you, will be a vast additional incitement; if that there be a future state, the hope of a happy existence in that, increases the appetite to deserve it: if that Jesus was also a God, you will be comforted by a belief of his aid and love. In fine, I repeat, you must lay aside all prejudice on both sides, and neither believe nor reject anything, because any other person or description of persons, have rejected or believed it. *Your own reason is the only oracle given you by heaven, and you are answerable not for the rightness, but uprightness of the decision.* (*Jefferson's Memoirs*, vol. ii. pp. 216–18.)

In another place, Jefferson writes to Dr Rush:

I am averse to the communication of my religious tenets to the public; because it would countenance the presumption of those who have endeavoured to draw them before that tribunal, and to seduce public opinion to erect itself into that inquisition over the rights of conscience, which the laws have so justly proscribed. *It behoves every man who values liberty of conscience for himself, to resist invasions of it in the case of others;* or their case may, by change of circumstances, become his own. It behoves him too, in his own case, to give no example of concession, *betraying the common right of independent opinion,* by answering questions of faith, which the laws have left between God and himself. (*Jefferson's Memoirs*, vol. iii. p. 515)

Mr Moore makes his friend 'answerable for the *rightness* of the decision' and as far as in him lies, 'invades the liberty of conscience in others', and 'betrays the common right of independent opinion'.

Of Matthews, Mr Moore writes thus:

Of this remarkable young man, Charles Skinner Matthews, I have already had occasion to speak, but the high station which he held in Lord Byron's affection and admiration, may justify a somewhat ampler tribute to his memory. There have seldom, perhaps, started together in life, so many youths of high promise and hope, as were to be found among the society of which Lord Byron formed a part at Cambridge. Of some of these, the names have since eminently distinguished themselves in the world, as the mere mention of Mr Hobhouse, and Mr William Bankes, is sufficient to testify; while in the instance of another of this lively circle, Mr Scrope Davies, the only regret of his friends is, that the social wit of which he is such a master, should, in the memories of his hearers alone, be likely to leave any record of its brilliancy. Among all these young men of learning and talent (including Byron himself, whose genius was, however, as yet 'an undiscovered world') the superiority, in almost every department of intellect, seems to have been, by the ready consent of all, awarded to Matthews; a concurrence of homage, which considering the persons from whom it came, gives such a high notion of the powers of his mind at that period, as renders the thought of what he might have been, if spared, a matter of interesting, though vain and mournful speculation. To mere mental pre-eminence, unaccompanied by the kindlier qualities of the heart, such a tribute, however deserved, might not perhaps have been so uncontestedly paid. But young Matthews appears, in spite of some little asperities of temper and manner, which he was already beginning to soften down when snatched away,—to have been one of those rare individuals who, while they command deference, can, at the same time, win regard, and who, as it were, relieve the intense feeling of admiration which they excite, by blending it with love.

To his religious opinions, and their unfortunate coincidence with those of Lord Byron, I have before adverted. Like his noble friend, ardent in the pursuit of truth, he, like him, had unluckily lost his way in seeking her, 'the light that led astray' being by both friends mistaken for hers. That in his scepticism he proceeded any further than Lord Byron, or ever suffered his doubting, but still ingenuous, mind to persuade itself into the 'incredible creed' of atheism, is I find, (notwithstanding an assertion in a letter of the noble poet to this effect) disproved by the testimony of those among his relations and friends, who are the most ready to admit, and of course lament, his other heresies; nor should I have felt that I had any right to allude thus to the religious opinions of one, who had never, by promulgating his heterodoxy, brought himself within the jurisdiction of the public, had not the wrong impression, as it appears, given of those opinions, on the authority of Lord Byron, rendered it an act of justice to both friends to remove the imputation. (pp. 277-9)

This passage contains several points worthy of remark: 1st, the highest possible panegyric on the moral and intellectual excellence of an individual, whose religious opinions were unfortunately like lord Byron's, though what lord Byron's opinions were, as we have just seen, Mr Moore does not know. 2nd, that Mr Moore himself can most clearly distinguish the light of truth from the light that leads astray, though he had the unkindness never to shew his friend a glimpse of the former, basking as he does in its meridian blaze. 3rd, that it is an act of justice to both friends to prove that one had grossly misrepresented the other. 4th, that the friends of Mr Matthews, *of course*, lament his heresies; they lament them as a matter of course.—Why, of course? There is nothing stated respecting them but that they were his friends. They might have agreed or disagreed with him. 'Of course,' says Mr Moore, they disagreed with him. Why *of course?* we repeat. There can be but one answer: because it is of course that Mr Moore should say of those he wishes to flatter just what he thinks the majority of his readers would wish to have said.

We next come to the following fantastical speculation about the poems to Thyrza:

It was about the time when he was bitterly feeling, and expressing, the blight, which his heart had suffered from a real object of affection, that his poems on the death of an imaginary one, 'Thyrza', were written; nor is it any wonder, when we consider the peculiar circumstances under which these beautiful effusions flowed from his fancy, that of all his strains of pathos, they should be the most touching and most pure. They were, indeed, the essence, the abstract spirit, as it were, of many griefs;—a confluence of sad thoughts from many sources of sorrow, refined and warmed in their passage through his fancy, and forming thus one deep reservoir of mournful feeling. In retracing the happy hours he had known with the friends now lost, all the ardent tenderness of his youth came back upon him.

His school-sports with the favourites of his boyhood, Wingfield and Tattersall—his summer days with Long, and those evenings of music and romance, which he had dreamed away in the society of his adopted brother, Eddlestone—all these recollections of the young and dead now came to mingle themselves in his mind with the image of her who, though living, was, for him, as much lost as they, and diffused that general feeling of sadness through his soul, which found a vent in these poems. No friendship, however warm, could have inspired sorrow so passionate, as no love, however pure, could have kept passion so chastened. It was the blending of the two affections in his memory and imagination, that thus gave birth to an ideal object combining the best features of both, and drew from him these saddest and tenderest of love-poems, in which we find all the depth and intensity of real feeling touched over with such a light as no reality ever wore. (pp. 302, 303)

This passage presents a curious instance of confusion of imagery:—A blight is felt: a blight is expressed: the heart suffers a blight from an object of affection: the effusions that flow from the fancy become touching and pure strains: these again become an essence, an abstract spirit: these are changed into a confluence of streams from many sources; and these, being refined and warmed, form a reservoir. Effusions, strains, essences, confluent streams, are all different and discrepant things; and though streams may fill a reservoir, they cannot form one. And, after all, depth and intensity are touched over with light. No doubt this is all very pretty, and sweetly sentimental.

A little further on in the volume is the following still more fantastical passage:

In all such speculations and conjectures as to what might have been, under more favourable circumstances, his character, it is invariably to be borne in mind, that his very defects were among the elements of his greatness, and that it was out of the struggle between the good and evil principles of his nature that his mighty genius drew its strength. A more genial and fostering introduction into life, while it would doubtless have softened and disciplined

his mind, might have impaired its vigour; and the same influence
that would have diffused smoothness and happiness over his life,
might have been fatal to its glory. In a short poem of his,* which
appears to have been produced at Athens (as I find it written on a
leaf of the original MS. of Childe Harold, and dated 'Athens,
1811') there are two lines which, though hardly intelligible as
connected with the rest of the poem, may, taken separately, be
interpreted as implying a sort of prophetic consciousness that it
was out of the wreck and ruin of all his hopes the immortality of
his name was to arise: —

> Dear object of defeated care,
> > Though now of love and thee bereft,
> To reconcile me with despair,
> > Thine image and my tears are left.
> 'Tis said with sorrow Time can cope,
> > But this I feel can ne'er be true;
> *For, by the death-blow of my hope,*
> > *My memory immortal grew!* (p. 323)

This is really curious. Here is a gentleman dabbling all his life
in poetry and criticism, and still incapable of seizing a meaning
so obvious, that it is most marvellous how any one could miss it.
By the death-blow of my hope: the blow that deprived me of the
original of this picture—*my memory grew immortal*: my remem-
brance of her became so strong that it shews not the slightest
symptom of decay; now, when after a lapse of time I look at her
picture, the painful feelings of memory are as vivid as on the
day I lost her. This proves that 'Time cannot cope with sorrow'. Mr Moore, however, expounds the passage thus: *By the
death-blow of my hope* in the loss of this object, I laid the foundation of an *immortal memory* for myself: of my being immor-
tally remembered. This proves that 'Time cannot cope with
sorrow'. A most contorted interpretation, and a most exemplary
non sequitur.

This specimen of Mr Moore's method of understanding his
friend's poetry speaks very ill for the sort of selection he has
been likely to make from his remains.

---

* Written beneath the picture of ———.

The publication of Childe Harold—the non-publication of Hints from Horace, an imitation of the Art of Poetry—the manner in which Mr Moore *scraped acquaintance* with Lord Byron (a phrase which we use designedly, because we find it so felicitously illustrated in this very curious procedure)—the history of Lord Byron's life at Newstead and in London—the publication of the Giaour, Bride of Abydos, and Corsair—his marriage with Miss Milbanke, the daughter of Sir Ralph Noel Milbanke, on the 2nd of January, 1815—his share in the management of Drury Lane Theatre—his separation from his wife in January, 1816—and his final departure from England on the 25th of April, 1816, are the principal events recorded in the remainder of this volume. No new light, as we have said, is thrown upon anything about which the public curiosity had been strongly excited: but there is a great deal of detail about minute corrections of the press, about alterations and re-alterations in that very important theatrical state-paper, the Address for the opening of Drury Lane Theatre; a great deal of gossip about all sorts of people, much that should not have been published, and more that is not worth publishing; some peeps behind the curtain of the Edinburgh Review, for which the parties principally implicated in that shallow and dishonest publication will scarcely thank the exhibitor; a few things said, and many hinted, about Lord Byron's amours; a few touches on the politics of Lord Byron and his biographer; and a speculation by Mr Moore about the usual unhappiness of intellectual persons in marriage.

The gossip about individuals is given with one or two peculiarities worthy of note. An initial is given in one page which sets the reader guessing; a name is given in another which saves him the trouble; or circumstances are so detailed as to point to the name unerringly. In one page we find 'Bold W.' going to be thrown out of a window; in another we find a friendly mention of 'Bold Webster'. A gentleman who sometimes neglects to send remittances is always Mr H.: a gentleman who sometimes sends them is always Mr Hanson. In one place

Lord Byron sees S * * *'s mistress and her mother in an opposite box at the theatre; and who S * * *'s mistress was is indicated a dozen lines lower:

> Went to my box at Covent-Garden to-night; and my delicacy felt a little shocked at seeing S * * *'s mistress (who, to my certain knowledge, was actually educated from her birth for her profession) sitting with her mother, 'a three-piled b——d, b——d-major to the army,' in a private box opposite. I felt rather indignant; but, casting my eyes round the house, in the next box to me, and the next, and the next, were the most distinguished old and young Babylonians of quality—so I burst out a laughing. It was really odd; lady * * divorced—lady * *, and her daughter, lady * *, both divorceable—Mrs * *, in the next, the like, and still nearer * * * * * *! What an assemblage to me, who know all their histories. It was as if the house had been divided between your public and your understood courtesans; but the intriguantes much outnumbered the regular mercenaries. On the other side were only Pauline and her mother, and, next box to her, three of inferior note. Now, where lay the difference between her and her mamma, and lady * * and daughter? except that the two last may enter Carleton and any other house, and the two first are limited to the opera and b—— house. How I do delight in observing life as it really is!—and myself, after all, the worst of any. But, no matter—I must avoid egotism, which, just now, would be no vanity. (p. 470)

Now as there were only one mother and daughter opposite, and as they were Pauline and her mother, S * * *'s mistress was Pauline. Who S * * * was, is therefore as clear as if his name had been printed. The volume abounds with these mockeries of reserve.

In other cases, and there is an instance in the last-cited passage, asterisks only are given, which communicate nothing. The following is another instance:

> To-morrow there is a party of purple at the 'blue' Miss * * *'s. Shall I go? Um!—I don't much affect your blue-bottles; but one ought to be civil. There will be ('I guess now,' as the Americans say), the Staëls and Mackintoshes—good—the * * *s and * * *s—not so good—the * * *s, &c., &c.—good for nothing. Perhaps that

> blue-winged Kashmirian butterfly of book-learning, lady ***,
> will be there. I hope so; it is a pleasure to look upon that most
> beautiful of faces. (p. 458)

What can be the possible use of printing such passages? Sometimes we have things in this way:

> P.S. Oh! the anecdote! ****************. (p. 558)

The extreme folly of such a specimen of publication is really
sufficiently ludicrous to amount to an excellent jest. Oh! the
anecdote, indeed! This should stand at the head of anecdotes of
book-making, if ever Sholto and Reuben Percy take them in
hand.

We shall cite two passages which throw a little light on the
politics of Lord Byron, and still more on those of his biographer:

> It was at this time that Lord Byron became acquainted (and, I
> regret to have to add, partly through my means) with Mr Leigh
> Hunt, the editor of the well-known weekly journal, the Examiner.
> This gentleman I had myself formed an acquaintance with in the
> year 1811, and, in common with a large portion of the public, en-
> tertained a sincere admiration of his talents and courage as a
> journalist. The interest I took in him personally had been recently
> much increased by the manly spirit which he had displayed
> throughout a prosecution instituted against himself and his
> brother, for a libel that had appeared in their paper on the Prince
> Regent, and in consequence of which they were both sentenced to
> imprisonment for two years. It will be recollected that there
> existed among the Whig party, at this period, a strong feeling of
> indignation at the late defection from themselves and their prin-
> ciples of the illustrious personage, who had been so long looked
> up to as the friend and patron of both. Being myself, at the time,
> warmly,—perhaps intemperately,—under the influence of this
> feeling, I regarded the fate of Mr. Hunt with more than common
> interest, and, immediately on my arrival in town, paid him a visit
> in his prison. On mentioning the circumstance, soon after, to
> Lord Byron, and describing my surprise at the sort of luxurious
> comforts with which I had found the wit in the dungeon sur-
> rounded,—his trellised flower-garden without, and his books,
> busts, pictures, and piano-forte within,—the noble poet, whose

political views of the case coincided entirely with my own, expressed a strong wish to pay a similar tribute of respect to Mr
Hunt, and accordingly, a day or two after, we proceeded for that
purpose to the prison. The introduction which then took place
was soon followed by a request from Mr Hunt that we would dine
with him, and the noble poet having good-naturedly accepted the
invitation, the Cold Bath Fields prison had, in the month of June,
1813, the honour of receiving Lord Byron, as a guest, within its
walls. (pp. 400, 401)

It was, we believe, in Horsemonger-Lane gaol, and not in that
of Cold-Bath-Fields, that Mr Leigh Hunt was imprisoned.
Mr Moore is too genteel to know one gaol from another. But it
appears that Mr Moore's patriotic sympathy was aroused on
this occasion, not by the specific case of oppression, but by its
coincidence with the Prince Regent's defection from the Whigs.
If the Whigs had been in place, Mr Hunt, as a part of the
arrangement, might have been very properly in gaol. If Mr
Moore should say, the Whigs would not have sent him there,
let our present Whig attorney-general answer him for us. It is
always, *quo, non quomodo*, with Mr Moore. His movement to the
state prison was not a patriotic, nor a philosophic, nor a philan-
thropic, movement. It was a Whig movement. He has thought
proper to apologize for it, and we have translated his apology
into plain English.

The second passage is this:

On the second of June, in presenting a petition to the House of
Lords, he made his third and last appearance as an orator, in that
assembly. In his way home from the House that day, he called, I
remember, at my lodgings, and found me dressing in a very great
hurry for dinner. He was, I recollect, in a state of most humourous
exaltation after his display, and, while I hastily went on with my
task in the dressing-room, continued to walk up and down the
adjoining chamber, spouting forth for me, in a sort of mock-
heroic voice, detached sentences of the speech he had just been
delivering. 'I told them,' he said, 'that it was a most flagrant violation of the constitution—that, if such things were permitted,
there was an end of English freedom, and that—' 'But what is this
dreadful grievance?' I asked, interrupting him in his eloquence.
'The grievance?' he repeated, pausing as if to consider—'Oh, that

I forget.'* It is impossible, of course, to convey an idea of the dramatic humour with which he gave effect to these words, but his look and manner on such occasions were irresistibly comic, and it was, indeed, rather in such turns of fun and oddity than in any more elaborate exhibition of wit that the pleasantry of his conversation existed. (p. 402)

A man in earnest would not have spoken in parliament about a grievance, without believing that the thing spoken of was a grievance. A man in earnest would not, having spoken of a public grievance in parliament, have afterwards professed to forget what the grievance was. A man, whether in earnest or not himself, would not, in speaking to a man whom he believed to be in earnest, have treated his own advocacy of public grievances as a jest. Lord Byron would not have spoken in this strain to Mr Shelley. And a man, whose own political opinions were anything but a farce, would not record an anecdote, so discreditable to both parties, as a mere piece of pleasantry, and nothing more.

The only political affairs about which Lord Byron seems to have felt any real and earnest interest, within the period here recorded, were those of Napoleon. He concluded a journal which he had kept for some time, and from which Mr Moore has given ample extracts, in these words:

April 19th, 1814.—There is ice at both poles, north and south— all extremes are the same—misery belongs to the highest and the lowest only,—to the emperor and the beggar, when unsixpenced and unthroned. There is, to be sure, a damned insipid medium— an equinoctial line—no one knows where, except upon maps and measurement.

> And all our yesterdays have lighted fools
> The way to dusty death.

I will keep no further journal of that same hesternal torch-light; and, to prevent me from returning, like a dog, to the vomit of memory, I tear out the remaining leaves of this volume, and write

---

* This speech was on presenting a Petition from Major Cartwright.

in Ipecacuanha, that the Bourbons are restored!!! Hang up philosophy. To be sure, I have long despised myself and man, but I
never spat in the face of my species before — 'O fool! I shall go
mad.' (pp. 513, 514)

Lord Byron wished to serve Mr Coleridge. He persuaded
Mr Murray to publish *Christabel*. He tried, through Mr Moore,
to persuade Mr Jeffrey to review it favourably in the Edinburgh
Review. But Mr Jeffrey knew better than to compromise the
character of his publication, by giving a true and just account
of any literary work, even to please his new friend Lord Byron.
This most beautiful little poem was therefore consigned to the
hands of that one of Mr Jeffrey's coadjutors, who combined the
most profound ignorance, and the grossest obtuseness of intellect, with the most rancorous malignity, and the most unblushing literary dishonesty. The Edinburgh Review has furnished many specimens of all these qualities: but in this article
on Coleridge's *Christabel*, they were all combined in the most
striking degree. Every thing was garbled, falsified, distorted,
misrepresented. The Review has not destroyed Mr Coleridge's
poetical fame: that was, and is, beyond its reach: but it destroyed his chance of popularity by extinguishing curiosity towards his poem at the time of its publication, at a time especially, when to have assisted him to that share of public attention
which he has always merited as a poet, would, though nothing
more than an act of justice, have had the effect of an act of
generosity. Of course, neither was to be expected from the
Edinburgh Review.

We must say a word or two more about Mr Moore's figures.
The following is a curious specimen:

> There is a healthfulness in the moral feeling so unaffectedly
> expressed in this letter, which seems to answer for a heart sound
> at the core, however passion might have scorched it. (pp. 231, 232)

What is the relation between scorching and a sound core? Half
the metaphor is from a rotten apple, and half from a roasted one.
Mr Moore never produces a figure that will stand the test of

analysis. His figures are all made up of disparates and non-existences. We do not know in all his writings, a single exception to this rule. The more his images are examined, the more unreal and incoherent they appear. Throughout the present work, he seems often to aim at simplicity: a good aim, but not easily attainable by one who has so long indulged in the rhetoric of false sentiment. He writes figures in spite of himself, and the only result of his endeavour at a simple and natural style is, that, by not fixing his attention on any predominant image, he makes his figurative language more than ever chaotic and caleidoscopical. We will give one example taken at random.

> When we look back to the *unbridled career*, of which his marriage was meant to be the *goal*, — to the *rapid and restless course* in which his life had *run along*, like a *burning train*, through a *series* of wanderings, adventures, successes and passions, the *fever* of all which was still upon him, when, with the same *headlong* recklessness, he *rushed* into this marriage — it can but little surprise us, that in the space of one short year, he would not have been able to recover all at once from his *bewilderment*, or to *settle down* into that tame *level* of conduct which the officious spies of his privacy required. As well might it be expected that a *steed* like his own Mazeppa's, should stand still, when reined, without *chafing* or *champing the bit*. (pp. 649, 650)

What a chaos with horses, goals, fire-trains, fevers, levels, and bewilderments! And this is about the ordinary style of the work.

The volume contains many allusions to persons who have never obtruded themselves on public notice, and whose names and circumstances ought not to have been dragged before the world. It is, on the whole, a production little instructive to the reader, little creditable to the author, little honourable to its subject: a speculation, perhaps a profitable one, on the public appetite for gossip, backed by a systematical deference to every widely-diffused prejudice, and to every doctrine and opinion which the influential classes of readers desire to be popular. And amongst these classes, the influential in the press are by no means forgotten. The 'great talents' of Mr Thomas Barnes, of the Times; the 'ingenious and remarkable' Mr Hogg, of Blackwood's Magazine; the 'most gifted of critics', Mr Jeffrey, and so forth, receive, and of course repay, the meed of just and discriminating praise.

> Discedo Alcæus puncto illius. Ille meo quis?
> Quis, nisi Callimachus?

We shall, for the reasons assigned in the commencement or this article, postpone our observations on the personal character of Lord Byron, and on some other matters, till we have gone through the second volume. Amongst the other matters, we include the whole of his amours, and the illustrations of the morality of the higher classes in this country, which his adventures and correspondence afford.

We have given very fair specimens of the matter and manner of the volume before us, and an outline of its contents, with such remarks as were imperiously demanded from us by our sense of the moral duty of exhibiting to our readers the real scope and purpose of a series of shallow sophisms and false assumptions, wrapped up in bundles of metaphors, put forth with a specious semblance of reason and liberality, and directed to the single end of upholding all abuses and delusions by which the aristocracy profit. In the second volume, Mr Moore will be on more perilous ground. To do justice to his friends who are gone, and to please those among the living, whose favour he most studiously courts in his writings, must be, in the treatment of that period which his second volume will embrace, impossible. He will endeavour to do both, after his fashion: and we think we can pretty accurately anticipate the result.

JEFFERSON'S
MEMOIRS

JEFFERSON'S MEMOIRS*

THIS is one of the most important publications ever presented to the world. In the catalogue of the benefactors of mankind, few deserve so high a station as Thomas Jefferson. As the author of the Declaration of Independence, and as one of the principal movers of the North American Revolution, his claims on the gratitude and admiration of posterity are divided with Washington, Franklin, and others, so excellent in their respective spheres, that it might be difficult, and would certainly be invidious, to say which was the most wise, the most disinterested, the most persevering in the perilous, and, at times, almost hopeless path, of arduous and self-devoting duty. But American liberty was destined to a second, scarcely less perilous, though less conspicuous struggle; a struggle in which there were no wounds, and guns, and drums, to fix the attention of Europe; but one in which the best energies of feeling and thought were necessary to save the United States from the effects of the vague terrors, with which many of their well-meaning citizens were inspired by the excesses of the French Revolution; and which, being worked on with all the arts of persuasion, by a large and influential party, in possession, for a time, of the government, who saw, or professed to see, no safety or permanence for political institutions, but in a government of corrupt influence, had

---

* *Memoirs, Correspondence, and Private Papers of Thomas Jefferson, late President of the United States.* Now first published from the original Manuscripts. Edited by Thomas Jefferson Randolph. 4 vols., 1829, Colburn and Bentley.

very nearly thrown the young republic into the arms of something very like our own happy aristocratical constitution. The good sense of the bulk of the people preserved them from this blessing; but the main glory of the signal victory over the domestic enemy belongs, on this occasion, undividedly to Jefferson.

The doctrines of anarchy and confusion, as they were called here; the doctrines against which, under the watchword of 'social order' and shouts 'for God and the King', we fired away in thirty years nearly three thousand millions of money in gunpowder, including the cost of the machinery, animate and inanimate, by which the said gunpowder was borne over land and sea for the final purposes of ignition, rarefaction, expansion, and explosion; the doctrines of the right of the possessors of life and property to choose for themselves the legislators who dispose of that life and property; of the right of the governed to discuss fully and freely, in censure as in praise, the public measures of their rulers, and the principles of their political and religious institutions; these doctrines were brought at once and efficiently into action on the accession of Jefferson to the Presidency, and 'the dissolution of social order', which our fire-and-sword logicians so long and confidently preached as the infallible consequence of the establishment of such maxims of government, consisted in the total abolition of internal taxes, in the rapid extinction of national debt, in the preservation of peace with all the world, in the bloodless acquisition of the important territory of Louisiana, and the complete possession of the Mississippi, in the efficient protection and ample reward of domestic industry, and in the establishment, beyond the reach of injury from the combined despotisms of the earth, of an asylum for the oppressed and unfortunate of all nations.

*   *   *

Our limits do not admit of our doing justice, in the form of extracts, to the invaluable contents of these volumes, of which we have given an imperfect enumeration. We have under some of the heads of that enumeration subjoined some brief specimens: but we most earnestly commend the volumes themselves to all our readers who have not yet perused them, as containing numerous and rich materials of authentic history; as presenting, on almost all truly important questions, views sometimes new, most frequently just, and always worthy of patient consideration; as abounding with incitements to moral courage and political honesty; as confirming rational hopes of the progress of knowledge and liberty; as elevating our opinion of human nature; and in all these points counteracting the soul-withering influence of our own frivolous and sycophantic literature.

America is deeply indebted to Jefferson. He had the sagacity to see her true interests in the beginning of his career, the honesty to sacrifice all other considerations to them, and the moral courage to pursue them inflexibly to the end. And the interests of America being peace and liberty, were and still are the interests of mankind. He was a great instrument in the foundation of her liberties in 1776; the main instrument in their restoration in 1800. He lived to see the community of which he was a member, proceed from infancy to maturity: he lived to see it rise from a struggle in which it with difficulty maintained its existence, to grow strongly and rapidly into one of the most noble and important communities of the world; and he left it in a fair train for becoming the very greatest of the nations. For how much of this progress it was indebted to him, will be most clearly manifest to those who dwell most on the history of his times, especially on the portion of them which intervened between that scarecrow of well-meaning simplicity, the French Reign of Terror, and his first election to the Presidency. The first steps of his administration dissipated for ever the phantoms of fear and delusion, with which artifice and cowardice had surrounded the image of liberty; and established principles of government, which remain to this day, not only unshaken, but apparently taking deeper and deeper hold of the affections of the

American people. He was undoubtedly the greatest public benefactor that has yet appeared in the nineteenth century; whatever may be his station in the eighteenth, in which it is difficult to say that he was second, even to Washington.

ESSAYS
ON MUSICAL
SUBJECTS

PAGANINI

PAGANINI is the great wonder of the day. It is a dispute among the learned (for which we refer to divers tractates *De Musica Veterum*), whether the tensile instruments of the ancients were all played by the hand, or whether some of them, of which the form seems well adapted to the purpose, were not played by the bow. We have hitherto been sceptical on this point; the evidence adduced by the partizans of the ancient bow has appeared to us shadowy and inconclusive: but, having heard Paganini, we are now satisfied that Orpheus and Amphion played on the violin, and that Paganini, having launched his bark into 'Cecilia's world of sound', has discovered, what is to us a new land, but in truth only the lost land of the ancients, the Atlantis of musical magic.

Paganini draws forth from his instrument notes and combinations which (in the modern world) none before him have produced or dreamed of: wild and wonderful alike in the strongest bursts of power, and in the softest and sweetest touches, air-drawn and evanescent as the voices of distant birds. The triumph of mechanical skill, astonishing as it is in itself, is the smallest part of the wonder. The real magic is not the novelty of the feat, but the surpassing beauty of the effect. It is the same with his performance on the single string (the fourth, or G string), as with his performance on four. New and surprising as is every part of the process, none of the phenomena of his execution appear to be exhibited for the sake of their own display: they appear as means, not ends. Novelty, of course, enters into the charm of the effect: but the great charm lies deeper than novelty: the perception of surpassing beauty would remain, if that of rarity and strangeness were withdrawn. It is this transcendent beauty and effect, that hushes his crowded audiences into an attention more profound than we ever witnessed in this usually gossiping theatre. The stillness was so deep, on the night of his first concert, that a single piece of wax, dropping from the side of a candle on the stage, had an effect absolutely startling: and this silence, contrasted strangely with the equally unprecendented tumult of applause, which burst forth at the close of his performance, accompanied by the unusual spectacle of the flourishing of hats, and the waving of handkerchiefs by ladies in the boxes.

Paganini is, to appearance, about forty-five; in person tall and thin, with long arms and long fingers—long black hair, parted on the forehead, and flowing back on the shoulders: small, and usually half-closed, eyes; a stupendous Roman nose; a tapering chin; a narrow and pale face, bearing traces of long and habitual ill-health; a figure that would be uncouth, if copied: manners that would be grotesque, if imitated—but both agreeable, and even graceful, from their natural and unaffected simplicity. He stands up, between the lamps and the orchestra, which is arranged on the stage, and plays, without written notes, music of his own composition, which seems to be the result of the inspiration of the moment, and which is replete with intellect and feeling—as if his mind were an inexhaustible treasury of deep thoughts and thrilling emotions, which he was pouring forth through the medium of 'all sweet sounds and harmonies'.

BEETHOVEN

BEETHOVEN'S *Fidelio* is the absolute perfection of dramatic music. It combines the profoundest harmony with melody that speaks to the soul. It carries to a pitch scarcely conceivable the true musical expression of the strongest passions, and the gentlest emotions, in all their shades and contrasts. The playfulness of youthful hope, the heroism of devoted love, the rage of the tyrant, the despair of the captive, the bursting of the sunshine of liberty upon the gloom of the dungeon, which are the great outlines of the feelings successively developed in this opera, are portrayed in music, not merely with truth of expression as that term might be applied to other works, but with a force and reality that makes music an intelligible language, possessing an illimitable power of pouring forth thought in sound. *Fidelio* is, we believe, Beethoven's only opera. It is the sun among the stars. It is not a step in the progress of dramatic music. It is a clear projection of it, a century in advance of its march.

This opera has been performed in a manner worthy of itself. Madame Schroeder Devrient possesses every requisite of the highest order for the lyrical stage. Her action is perfect nature. Her voice is sweet, clear, powerful, flexible; and above all, it is, both in speaking and singing, more pathetic and heart-touching than any we ever heard. Her intonation is unexceptionably true: her execution is at once highly finished, and of the most beautiful simplicity. The other characters are well sustained. The chorus is admirable. Each individual of it is an actor, discriminated in costume, in the business of the scene,

177

and in the distribution of the music. They sing together, or in parts, with a precision, an expression, a real share and interest in what is going on, to which there has been no parallel in this country. The chorus of prisoners emerging into daylight may alone be taken as a model of what a chorus ought to be.

MOZART

THERE is nothing perfect in this world except Mozart's music. Criticism has nothing to do with it, but to admire. Whatever is is right. Mozart cannot even be disparaged by comparison with himself—the detractor cannot say, 'How inferior this thing is to that!' for every composition seems to have a peculiar appropriateness to the occasion, and it is impossible to conceive any thing more suitable. There is nothing of mannerism in Mozart's music, and yet it cannot be mistaken for any other, or any other for it—it is peculiar in its excellence. The signature of the master is in an exalted sweetness of turns. In Mozart's operas there is every variety of style and expression, each having a marked style to which the varieties within it are subordinate and tributary. *Don Giovanni* and the *Zauberflöte* are both romantic operas, but of what different characters! In each the grandeur is relieved with gaiety; and here again how different the gaiety! In *Giovanni* it is touched with riot, in the *Zauberflöte* it is all fanciful and cheery. As wide a distinction is to be marked between the gaiety of *Figaro* and of *Cosi fan tutte;* the first is of enjoyment, the other the light laugh of the world coming more from the brain than the blood. The expression of the serious passions has as much variety in the works of Mozart as the comic. The simple sustained style of the *Clemenza* has no likeness in any of the solemn passages of his romantic operas, and the grandeur of the *Zauberflöte* is as distinguishable from the grandeur of *Giovanni,* as the devotional from the terrible. In the expression of tenderness there is most sameness in Mozart's compositions; and how could it be other than same while true to nature, which, in all states, shows herself much alike in the melting mood?

LORD MOUNT EDGCUMBE'S
MUSICAL REMINISCENCES*

THE first edition of this work was published seven or eight years ago; but being brought down to the present time, we may regard it as a new publication.

The Italian Opera is an affair that wants reforming; but after the signal failure of a professing reformer, three seasons ago, no one will again make the profession for fifty years to come with the slightest chance of obtaining belief that the promise will be fulfilled.

Lord Mount Edgcumbe's Reminiscences extend over a period of sixty years—a term nearly equivalent to one-half of the entire existence of the Italian Opera in England; and in the conclusion of them he thinks that, in every point of view—music, poetry, singers, audience—the Italian theatre in England has changed for the worse. 'First impressions,' he says, 'are the most lasting.' This is true; and they are also the most agreeable. There is no one object to which we have attached sufficient interest to make it an uniform pursuit, of which we may not say with Byron:

> No more, no more, oh! never more on me
> The freshness of the heart can fall like dew,
> Which, out of all the lovely things we see,
> Extracts emotions beautiful and new,

---

* *Musical Reminiscences; containing an Account of the Italian Opera in England from 1773.* 4th edit. Continued to the present time, and including the Festival in Westminster Abbey. By the Earl of Mount Edgcumbe. London: Andrews, 1834. pp. 294.

> Hived in our bosoms like the bag o' the bee.
>   Think'st thou the honey with those objects grew?
> Alas! 'twas not in them, but in thy power
> To double e'en the sweetness of a flower.

Herein lies the foundation of the *laudatio temporis acti,* which is inseparable from advancing years in all cases but in that of the philosophical few, who are satisfied that 'every generation grows wiser and wiser', and that the progress of the useful in one way is more than a compensation for the loss of the agreeable in another. We shall not discuss in this place how far the useful and agreeable are identical or opposite. Medicine is useful, and not agreeable; and it may, at some periods, be very desirable for the ultimate benefit of mankind that they should be subjected to a course of moral and political medicine, drenched with mental cathartics, and restricted, for their greatest indulgence, to potations of intellectual toast and water. This we shall not gainsay; but our present business is with an article of mental luxury, in which we shall restrict our view of the useful to that which is useful for the accomplishment of the object proposed, leaving the great question *de finibus* to those who have already settled it to their own satisfaction.

The object proposed by the Italian Opera is to present the musical drama in the most perfect possible form. To this end there must be, in the first place, a good drama: an interesting story, intelligibly told in good poetry, and affording ample scope for strong and diversified expression: good music, adapting the sound to the sense, and expressing all the changes and trains of feeling that belong to the ideas and images of the drama: good performers—persons of good figures and features —picturesque in action, and expressive in countenance—with voices of fine tone and great power, having true intonation, scientific execution, and above all, or rather as the crown of all, expression—expression—expression: the one all-pervading and paramount quality, without which dramatic music is but as a tinkling cymbal: elegant and appropriate dresses—beautiful scenery—a chorus, each of whom should seem as if he knew

that he had some business of his own in the scene, and not as if
he were a mere unit among thirty or forty automata, all going
like clock-work by the vibrations of the conductor's pendulum:
a full orchestra of accomplished musicians, with a good leader—
and especially without a conductor keeping up, in the very
centre of observation, a gesticulation and a *tapage* that make
him at once the most conspicuous and most noisy personage in
the assembly, distracting attention from the sights and sounds
that ought exclusively to occupy it—an affliction to the eye, and
a most pestilent nuisance to the ear. But, with all this, there
should be (as there used to be) an audience regulating its costume and its conduct by the common conventional courtesies
of evening society; not with men wearing hats among well-
dressed women, and rubbing dirty boots against white petticoats; nor with an influx of late comers, squeezing themselves
between the crowded benches, and sitting down in the laps of
their precursors, as we have both seen and suffered. We are
aware that some advocates for universal liberty think that the
morning liberty of the streets should be carried into all evening
assemblies; but, looking back to the Athenians, we cannot consider that cleanliness and courtesy are incompatible with the
progress of freedom and intelligence.

Now, by following out the principal points which we have
enumerated a little in detail, we shall see what we have had, and
what we have wanted—what we are likely to have, and what we
are likely to continue to want—for the bringing together of the
constituent portions of a perfect musical drama. Lord Mount
Edgcumbe touches all these points. We shall content ourselves,
on the present occasion, with citing a few of his observations,
and expressing our own opinions in a subsequent commentary:

> The opera in England, for the period of ten years after the
> departure of Catalani, will afford much less room for observation
> than any of the preceding, as far as the singers are concerned; for,
> with one or two exceptions, there were not any of whom I feel
> inclined to say much, because there is not much to be said in their
> praise. But so great a change has taken place in the character of the

dramas, in the style of the music, and in its performance, that I cannot help enlarging a little on that subject before I proceed farther.

One of the most material alterations is, that the grand distinction between serious and comic operas is nearly at an end, the separation of the singers for their performance entirely so. Not only do the same sing in both, but a new species of drama has arisen, a kind of mongrel between them, called *semi-seria*, which bears the same analogy to the other two that that non-descript the melo-drama does to the legitimate tragedy and comedy of the English stage. The construction of these newly-invented pieces is essentially different from the old. The dialogue, which used to be carried on in recitative, and which in Metastasio's operas is often so beautiful and interesting, is now cut up (and rendered unintelligible if it were worth listening to) into *pezzi concertati*, or long singing conversations, which present a tedious succession of unconnected, ever-changing motivos, having nothing to do with each other, and if a satisfactory air is for a moment introduced, which the ear would like to dwell upon to hear modulated, varied, and again returned to, it is broken off before it is well understood or sufficiently heard, by a sudden transition into a totally different melody, time, and key, and recurs no more: so that no impression can be made, or recollection of it preserved. Single songs are almost exploded, for which one good reason may be given, that there are few singers capable of singing them. Even a prima donna, who would formerly have complained at having less than three or four airs allotted to her, is now satisfied with one trifling cavatina for a whole opera.

The acknowledged decline of singing in general (which the Italians themselves are obliged to confess) has no doubt, in a great measure, occasioned this change. But another cause has certainly contributed to it, and that is the difference of the voices of the male performers. Sopranos have long ceased to exist, but tenors for a long while filled their place. Now even these have become so scarce, that Italy can produce no more than two or three very good ones. The generality of voices are basses, which, for want of better, are thrust up into the first characters, even in serious operas, where they used only to occupy the last place, to the manifest injury of melody, and total subversion of harmony, in which the lowest part is their peculiar province.

These new first singers are called by the novel appellation of *basso cantante* (which, by the bye, is a kind of apology, and an acknowledgment that they ought not to sing), and take the lead in

operas with almost as much propriety as if the double bass were
to do so in the orchestra, and play the part of the first fiddle. A
bass voice is too unbending, and deficient in sweetness for single
songs, and fit only for those of inferior character, or of the buffo
style. In duettos, it does not coalesce well with a female voice, on
account of the too great distance between them, and in fuller
pieces the ear cannot be satisfied without some good intermediate
voices to fill up the interval, and complete the harmony. Yet three
or four basses now frequently overpower one weak tenor, who
generally plays but a subordinate part. (pp. 118–23)

We shall begin with the drama itself—the dramatic poem, the
libretto. Rousseau has admirably described what the lyrical
drama ought to be:

> On sentit qu'il ne falloit a l'Opéra rien de froid et de raisonné,
> rien que le spectateur put écouter assez tranquillement pour
> réfléchir sur l'absurdité de ce qu'il entendoit; et c'est en cela
> surtout que consiste la différence essentielle du drame lyrique à
> la simple tragédie. Toutes les délibérations politiques, tous les
> projets de conspiration, les expositions, les récits, les maximes
> sentencieuses, en un mot, tout ce qui ne parle qu' à la raison, fut
> banni du langage du cœur, avec les jeux d'esprit, les madrigaux,
> et tout ce qui n'est que des pensées. Le ton même de la simple
> galanterie, qui cadre mal avec les grandes passions, fut a peine
> admis dans le remplissage des situations tragiques, dont il gâte
> presque toujours l'effet: car jamais on ne sent mieux que l'acteur
> chante, que lorsqu'il dit une chanson.

The business, indeed, of the lyrical dramatist is to present, with
the most perfect simplicity, the leading and natural ideas of
an impassioned action, divested of all imagery not arising from
spontaneous feeling. A heroine in distress must neither demonstrate her misery by an accumulation of evidence, as in an old
French tragedy, nor dress it out in a complication of heterogeneous figures, as in a modern English song, in which everything is illustrated by a chaos of images which never met in the
organized world: for instance, in a Venetian serenade, in the
opera of *Faustus*,

> Lucy dear, Lucy dear, wake to the spring,
> Hark! how the village bells merrily ring.

Village bells in Venice! and, moreover, peculiar to the spring—
a sort of tintinnabulary efflorescence, characteristic of the
season, like the cowslip and the cuckoo! Or in a song which we
have heard Braham sing fifty times,

> Is there a heart that never loved,
>   Or felt soft woman's sigh?
> Is there a man can mark unmoved
>   Dear woman's tearful eye?
> Go bear him to some desert shore,
>   Or solitary cell,
> Where none but savage monsters roar,
>   Where man ne'er deign'd to dwell.

Here is a solitary cell, of which the grievance is, not that none
dwell in it, but that none roar in it except savage monsters,
whose presence makes it solitary. Or in a song which we have
heard as often from half-a-dozen female singers,

> Meet me by moonlight alone,
>   And then I will tell you a tale
> Must be told by the moonlight alone,
>   In the grove at the end of the vale.
> You must promise to come, for I said
>   I would show the night-flowers their queen:
> Nay, turn not away that sweet head,
>   'Tis the loveliest ever was seen.

The reason for the lady meeting the gentleman by moonlight is,
that he has promised to show the night-flowers their queen,
videlicet herself; and the lady must do something very incon-
gruous, because the gentleman must keep his word with the
night-flowers.

We have put down these specimens from memory. They are
the first that occur to us, but they are fair samples of modern
English musical poetry—astounding and impertinent nonsense
—answering no purpose, if it happens to be heard, but to dis-
tract the attention from any degree of natural feeling and expression which may belong to the music or the voice. We had
much rather that the words were in the language of Otaheite.

We could then at least guess at something that suited the music.

The poetry of the Italian Opera is quite the contrary of all this. It gives, with little or no ornament, the language of passion in its simplest form: a clear and strong outline to be filled up by the music: which is itself the legitimate ornament and illustration of the leading ideas and sentiments of the scene. The essentials of style, in the composition of dramatic poetry for music, are simplicity and severity. It may be said, that the same rhymes and phrases are of constant recurrence; but though they are the same to read, they are not the same to hear. The *cor* and *amor*, *fedeltà* and *felicità* of *Desdemona* are not those of *Medea*. The music paints the difference. There is nothing in any Italian libretto at all resembling the egregious rigmarol of our modern English songs.

To illustrate what we have said, and to avoid even the appearance of selection, we will point to the words of Rubini's most popular airs: 'Ah! così ne'dì ridenti', and 'Vivi tu, te ne scongiuro' in *Anna Bolena*; 'Pasci il guardo' in *La Sonnambula*—and 'Tu vedrai la sventurata' in *Il Pirata*. We will quote a few lines from two of them:

> Nel veder la tua costanza
> Il mio cor si rasserena:
> Non temea che la tua pena,
> Non soffrì che il tuo soffrir.
> L' ultim' ora che s'avanza
> Ambidue sfidar possiamo,
> Che nessun quaggiù lasciamo
> Nè timore nè desir.
>
> *Anna Bolena.*

> Ma non fia sempre odiata
> La mia memoria, io spero;
> Se fui spietato e fiero,
> Fui sventurato ancor.
> E parlerà la tomba
> Alle pietose genti,
> De' lunghi miei tormenti,
> Del mio tradito amor.
>
> *Il Pirata.*

These are fair specimens of Italian airs, and serve to prove what we have alleged respecting the simplicity and even severity with which the leading ideas are presented unencumbered with ornament. Our old English songs were models of simplicity, but our modern songs are almost all false sentiment, overwhelmed with imagery utterly false to nature, like the night-flowers and solitary-celled monsters quoted above. Mr Moore, with his everlasting 'brilliant and sparkling' metaphors, has contributed to lead the *servum pecus* into this limbo of poetical vanity: but the original cause lies deeper: namely, in a very general diffusion of heartlessness and false pretension. We will not now pursue the investigation—but as we are speaking of English theatrical songs, we will observe, that the introduction, always objectionable, of airs not belonging to the piece, is nevertheless usually managed on the Italian stage with a certain degree of contrivance, and fitted by a new *scena* into the business of the drama. The same thing is done in English operas, in a manner marvellously clumsy and inartificial. For instance, Henry Bertram, in *Guy Mannering*, loses his way among rocks, expects to be attacked by thieves—resolves to fight manfully—recollects how manfully Nelson fought at Trafalgar, and strikes up—' 'Twas in Trafalgar bay!'

A singular instance of the obtuseness of our English opera song-makers occurs in the opera of *Rob Roy*. Some of Wordsworth's verses were adopted, including the well-known passage,

> the good old rule
> Suffices them; the simple plan,
> That they should take who have the power,
> And they should keep who can.

The opera-wright thought it would improve these verses to make the first and third lines rhyme, and actually altered them as follows:

> the good old maxim still
> Suffices them; the simple plan,
> That they should take who have the will,
> And they should keep who can.

He could not see the essential difference between the *will* and the *power* in this matter of taking.

Lord Mount Edgcumbe quotes a passage from Schlegel's Lectures:

> A few only of the operas of Metastasio still keep possession of the stage, as the change of taste in music demands a different arrangement of the text. Metastasio seldom has chorusses, and his airs are almost always for a single voice: with these the scenes uniformly terminate, and the singer never fails to make his exit with them. In an opera we now require more frequent duos and trios, and a *crashing* finale. In fact, the most difficult problem for the opera poet is the mixing the complicated voices of conflicting passions in one common harmony, without injuring their essence; a problem however which is generally solved by both poet and musical composer in a very arbitrary manner.

and adds,

> The consequence of this is that all the new dramas written for Rossini's music are most execrably bad, and contain scarcely one line that can be called poetry, or even one of common sense.

This sweeping condemnation is by no means merited. Some of Rossini's libretti are detestable enough; but there is much good dramatic poetry in some of them, *Tancredi* and *Semiramide* especially. It is true, that in these dramas the Italian poet had only to condense the essence of Voltaire's tragedies, but the task is well executed. The libretto of Donizetti's *Anna Bolena* is an excellent dramatic poem.

It is seldom that we are enabled to judge fairly either of an Italian libretto, or of the music of an opera as a whole. For example, in 1832 Mr Monck Mason professed to bring forward Pacini's *Gli Arabi nelle Gallie*. He first cut it into halves, and put the second half aside, or into the fire. He then cut away the beginning and substituted that of Rossini's *Zelmira*. He then tacked a strange air, we forget from whence, to the middle, by way of an end, and thus presented to the public both author and composer literally without head or tail. The critics discovered that the drama was nonsense, and that much of the music was stolen; and Pacini and his poet bore the blame which belonged to the manager. This mode of murdering reputations ought to subject the offender to an action for damages. 'I was induced, unfortunately,' says Lord Mount Edgcumbe, 'to go one night to see *Gli Arabi nelle Gallie*, a very poor opera by Pacini.' What he saw was poor enough, but it was not Pacini's opera. In the same season Bellini's *La Straniera*, which has much beautiful melody, and an interesting and intelligible story, founded on the Vicomte d'Arlincourt's *L'Etrangère*, was presented in such a chaotic fashion, that the intentions of both poet and composer remained an unfathomable mystery.

These liberties are taken more or less with the works of all masters, from the greatest to the least. Mozart himself does not escape them. Interpolation indeed he does escape. The audiences of the King's Theatre are justly strict in this one point only, that they will not permit the sewing on of an extraneous purple shred to any of his great and sacred textures. But garbled and mutilated his works are abominably, to fit the Procrustean bed of an inadequate company, or to quadrate with the manager's notions of the bad taste of the public. A striking instance of this is in the invariable performance of *Il Don Giovanni* without its concluding sestetto. Don Juan's first introduction to a modern English audience was in a pantomime (at Drury Lane we believe), which ended with the infernal regions, a shower of fire, and a dance of devils. Mozart's opera has, properly, no such conclusion. Flames arise—a subterranean chorus is heard— Don Juan sinks into the abyss—the ground closes above him— Leporello remains on the stage: a strongly-marked modulation leads from the key of D minor into that of G major, with a change from common time andante to triple time *allegro assai*; and the other characters, ignorant of the catastrophe, rush in to seek their revenge:

> Ah! dov' è il perfido,
> Dov' è l'indegno?

Leporello explains the adventure, and after a general exclama-

tion, a solemn pause, and an exceedingly sweet *larghetto* movement, in which the *dramatis personae* dispose of themselves, 'Or
che tutti, o mio tesoro,' the opera is wound up by a fugue in
D major—'Questo è il fin di chi fa mal': one of the very finest
things in dramatic music, and the most appropriate possible
termination of the subject; and yet is this most noble composition, this most fitting and genuine conclusion, sacrificed to a
dance of devils flashing torches of rosin, for no earthly reason
but that so ended the Drury Lane pantomime.

Le Nozze di Figaro and *Il Flauto Magico* both require a better
and more numerous company than is ever assembled in this
country. If we have in the former an Almaviva, a Figaro, a Con-
tessa and a Susanna, it is the usual extent of our good fortune.
We have seldom an endurable Cherubino; Marcellina is generally a nonentity: Barbarina always so; Bartolo, Basilio, and
Antonio take their chance, which is seldom good for any of them,
and never for all; and Don Curzio is for the most part abrogated.

Il Don Giovanni and *Le Nozze di Figaro* are both specimens
of excellently-written libretti, separating most effectively the
action and passion from the ratiocination of the originals; but
we have seen the latter especially performed in such a manner,
that if we had known nothing of it but from the representation,
we should have found it incomprehensible; and this sort of experiment on things which we know well should make us cautious
of pronouncing summary judgment on things of which we know
nothing but from the showing of the King's Theatre.

Il Flauto Magico is a well-written libretto, but the subject is
too mystical to be interesting, or even generally intelligible; and
this is a great drawback on its theatrical popularity, which has
never approached that of the *Giovanni* and *Figaro*, though the
music exhausts all the fascinations of both melody and harmony,
and may be unhesitatingly cited as the absolute perfection of
both. It requires more good singers than either of the others,
and it requires them the more imperatively, as it depends more
exclusively on the music. It requires seventeen voices besides
the chorus. The music which is assigned to the three nymphs

and the three genii is almost supernaturally beautiful: for this alone there should be six good voices, and there are, without these, six principal and five secondary parts. We may therefore despair of ever hearing this opera performed as it ought to be.

The works of Italian composers do not require, in any instance that we remember, so many performers. Those of the most modern composer of any name—Bellini—are singularly restricted in their principal parts. He seems to endeavour to defend himself against the caprices and jealousies of the performers by giving them nothing to quarrel about. A *prima soprano*, a *primo tenore*, a *primo basso*, and the ordinary components of a chorus, can perform his *Pirata*. There can be no dispute here about pre-eminence, but the general effect is necessarily meagre. But the progress of self-conceit among singers has made this result inevitable. A *prima soprano* is now to be found everywhere, and a *seconda* nowhere; and though many who assume to be first are scarcely fit to be second, they will not be content with what they are fit for, but will be first or nothing. There appears to be this great difference between a German and an Italian company—that the Germans will co-operate to the production of general effect, and the Italians will look to nothing but their own individual display. We have seen, in a German opera, the same person taking a principal part one night, and singing in the chorus the next. We have seen the same with the French; but with the Italians this never occurs. A German author and composer may therefore give fair scope to their subject; but the Italians must sacrifice everything to their company, and all in vain, except for the first production—for to the whims and inefficiency of every new company the unfortunate opera must be refitted and garbled. Bellini's is the true plan for his own reputation. A soprano, a tenor, a bass, and a chorus, there must be in every company, and they can have nothing to quarrel for; but the musical drama must be ruined if this were to become the rule of its construction. And the scheme, after all, is not always successful: for in 1830 the *prima donna* transposed the middle and end of *Il Pirata* in order that she might finish it herself instead of the tenor.

'Ma femme, et cinq ou six poupets' will not make a company in the opinion of any one but Catalani's husband. No one, indeed, who has seen and heard Catalani, or Pasta, or Malibran, or Giulietta Grisi, would willingly dispense with one such *prima donna*; but the single star should not be worshipped exclusively to the sacrifice of the general effect. She can be but a component, however important, part of it; and if the general effect fails, the star will fall.

But with us, though the star cannot shine if the general effect be bad, no general effect, however otherwise excellent, will produce attraction without a star. In 1832, though the star of the French opera of *Robert le Diable* (Madame Cinti) was but one of the fourth magnitude, yet with her eclipse the opera fell. We thought the general effect improved by the substitution of Mdlle Schneider, but the public resolutely abstained from sitting in judgment on the question. Madame Cinti's voice was not powerful—Mdlle Schneider's much less so: both had sweetness and good execution; but Madame Cinti was as cold as an icicle, and Mdlle Schneider was all feeling and expression. For example, in the Princess Isabella's duet with her lover Robert, in which he begins,

> Avec bonté voyez ma peine
>   Et mes remords,
> Et n'allez pas par votre haine
>   Punir mes torts,

the princess echoes the words, 'Et vos remords!' 'Punir vos torts!' In Madame Cinti's performance we had merely the musical echo: in Mdlle Schneider's we had an expression of the deepest tenderness. Her 'Et vos remords' seemed to imply that his remorse was an expiation of his offences: her 'Punir vos torts' seemed to imply, that for her to punish his offences was impossible. Now this is the expression which is the soul of music, of which Madame Cinti had not a particle, and of which Mdlle Schneider was full to overflowing; but everybody went to hear Madame Cinti, and nobody went to hear Mdlle Schneider. We formed our secret opinion in the solitude of an empty theatre, and now communicate it to the public in especial confidence.

We do not agree in opinion with Lord Mount Edgcumbe that the decline of singing in Italy has conduced to the composition of melodramas and the frequency of pezzi concertati. There has been an increase of excitement in the world of reality, and that of imagination has kept it company. The ordinary stage deserted the legitimate drama for melo-drama before the musical stage did so. The public taste has changed, and the supply of the market has followed the demand. There can be no question that Rossini's music is more spirit-stirring than Paësiello's, and more essentially theatrical: more suited to the theatre by its infinite variety of contrast and combination, and more dependent on the theatre for the development of its perfect effect. We were present at the first performance of an opera of Rossini's in England: *Il Barbiere di Siviglia*, in March, 1818. We saw at once that there was a great revolution in dramatic music. Rossini burst on the stage like a torrent, and swept everything before him except Mozart, who stood, and will stand, alone and unshaken, like the Rock of Ages, because his art is like Shakespeare's, identical with nature, based on principles that cannot change till the constitution of the human race itself be changed, and therefore secure of admiration through all time, as the drapery of the Greek statues has been through all the varieties of fashion.

Whether singing in Italy has declined is another question. Lord Mount Edgcumbe received his first impressions in the days of 'the divine Pacchierotti'. We, who received ours at a later period, cannot sympathize with him in his regret for the *musici*. We are content with such vocal music as the natural voice will allow us; we listen with unmixed pleasure to such a basso as Tamburini. The whole compass of the human voice finds its appropriate distribution in concerted music, otherwise the distribution is wrong, and not the principle of admitting

8

the bass voice. The *basso-cantante* does not take the lead in the *pezzo-concertato*, any more than the double bass takes the place of the first fiddle in the orchestra. The one has its proper place in the instrumental, and the other in the vocal distribution. And if much of the dialogue which was formerly carried on in recitative is now carried on in concerted music, it is because it is found more agreeable and more suited to the changes and varieties of passion, and is at the same time readily followed by the majority of the audience, who would now find an old opera consisting of only recitative and single airs, with at most one or two duets, or a duet and a *terzetto*, a very insipid production. The favourites of a century, or even half a century back, could not be successfully reproduced without *ripienimenti*.

Lord Mount Edgcumbe's first impressions make him partial to thin and shrill tones. This is evident to us, in his praise of Camporese and Caradori; but with the decline of the *musici*, a fuller volume of tone in the female voice has been more and more required to satisfy the ear in concert with *tenori* and *bassi*. Tosi, the idol of Naples, with her *soprano-sfogato* voice, was not endured in England in 1832. The perfection of our domestic musical instruments has also contributed to this result. We have lost all relish, and even all toleration, for the tone of the harpsi-chord, since we have received our first ideas from that of the piano-forte.

A good opera well performed is a great rarity with us. Good operas there are in abundance; but there are seldom either sense or knowledge in the management to select them, or power or good-will in the company to do them justice. The best singers come here for only a portion of the season: they sing morning, noon, and night, at concerts; they have no time to rehearse. The manager has collected stars, but not a company: there is a soprano too much, and a contralto too little—a tenor wanting, and a basso to spare: they patch up a performance as they may—altering, garbling, omitting, interpolating—and the result is, a bad concert instead of a good opera. A good opera is a whole, as much in the music as in the poetry, and

cannot be dislocated and disfigured by omissions and inter-
polations, without destruction to its general effect.

Lord Mount Edgcumbe justly observes that

> a mean economy prevails in all the inferior departments, with
> regard to secondary singers, the chorus and orchestra: the scenery,
> decorations, and wardrobe, are in every respect unworthy of the
> largest theatre in the country. (p. 176)

But the enormous expense of the principal singers and dancers
would not alone render this mean economy necessary, if it were
not for the enormous rent exacted for the house. By a rough
calculation which we made the other day, it appeared to us that
the Italian Opera has been carried on in England for about a
century and a quarter, at an average net loss of 5,000*l.* a year;
but of late years the Opera has yielded what would have been a
liberal profit to the proprietors of the theatre, if it had been
carried on by the proprietors, and not by a lessee, saddled with
a disproportionate rent.

Lord Mount Edgcumbe reprobates the novel introduction of
a conductor into the orchestra, not playing himself but beating
time with a noisy bâton. Assuredly our Italian opera conductor
verifies the remark of Dr Burney:

> Rousseau says, that the more time is beaten the less it is kept;
> and it is certain that when the measure is broken, the fury of the
> musical general, or director, increasing with the disorder and con-
> fusion of his troops, he becomes more violent, and his strokes and
> gesticulations more ridiculous in proportion to their disorder.
> (p. 235)

Lord Mount Edgcumbe makes some observations on the change
which has taken place in the appearance and conduct of the
audience of the King's Theatre, which we fully agree with him
is a change altogether for the worse. We confess we have a prejudice in favour of sitting at our ease among well-mannered
company, and we have been elbowed and annoyed out of all
endurance of the pit at the Opera. Amongst the principal
causes of this change is the profuse admission of orders; and

on what ground these are given we saw the other day some
curious evidence in a case in the Court of Requests. One of the
former managers of the Opera had set up a paper called the
Theatrical Critic, which did not succeed, and had left off in
debt to the editor two guineas, for which important amount he
was summoned; and it appeared that, in postponing the pay-
ment, he had told the editor a box was always at his service.
After this we need not wonder at the heterogeneous composition of the audience in the pit. Assuredly those who pay have a
right to complain, if they find all the places pre-occupied by
those who do not. They do not complain, however, but they
exercise another right more fatal to the management, and more
just to its misconduct—the right of staying away. In short, as
Lord Mount Edgcumbe justly observes,

> The whole system is radically bad; and nothing can restore the
> Opera in this country to its former respectable and agreeable foot-
> ing, or the performances to that excellence which a public paying
> so dearly has a right to expect, but a total reformation, and entire
> change of proprietors, of managers, of all parties connected with
> the theatre, I had almost said, hampered and embarrassed as it is,
> of the theatre itself (p. 168.)

We should be sorry to change the theatre, because it is the
finest vehicle for sound in Europe; but we wish to see it
thoroughly reformed in all the points to which we have adverted,
and in another very important matter—that of its exits and its
entrances. It was not intended for a crowd, but it is now often
crowded, legitimately or artificially; and the occurrence of a
fire on a crowded night would ensure the destruction of the
audience. It is surrounded, or rather built in, by shops and
taverns, and even the alarm of fire in any one of these would
occasion incalculable mischief.

But it is vain to anticipate any reform of this theatre while it
is in the hands of the assignees of a bankrupt estate, who think
only of exacting the utmost possible rent within the year—(a
double rent, in short: first, a fair return on the capital; and,
second, a most unfair and unjustifiable tax on the monopoly of

the license)—from an impresario who is only an annual tenant, who can, therefore, make no prospective arrangements—who is always taken unprovided at the beginning of the season—who thinks of nothing but how to make both ends meet at the end of it—who trusts to his skill in the 'detection of a star' to redeem himself by a temporary attraction in the course of it—and who, if he can fill the theatre by a fiddler or a dancer, is content to let the opera take its chance. It is true that we are indebted to him for some operatic stars, as well as for heroes of one string, and heroines of one toe; but he has done nothing, or worse than nothing, for the musical drama, about which he neither knows nor cares anything. Last year he had five admirable performers: Giulietta Grisi, Rubini, Tamburini, Ivanoff, and Zuchelli—the first three the best soprano, tenor and bass, perhaps, in the whole musical world. What these five could do was done transcendently well, but he had no contralto, or one too inefficient to be a principal, and too conceited to be a second; and *La Gazza Ladra* was performed a dozen times with a walking Pippo. Half a dozen most familiar operas, and one indifferent novelty, were the entire performances of the season: still it was much to have such singers, especially with the exquisite acting and personal fascinations of Giulietta Grisi, and they carried the season profitably through, with the help, indeed, of Taglioni, *la Déesse de la danse*. The present manager has an advantageous foil in the *impresario* of 1832, who, having professed to reform the Italian Opera, did not present a single good Italian performance throughout his entire management; but a manager of the Italian Opera should be

conversant with the Italian stage, a good judge of music and of singers, acquainted with foreign languages and foreign usages, of liberal ideas, not sparing of expense, but judicious in the application of it; knowing what is right, and firm in exercising his authority to enforce it: in short, one who can act for himself, and not be dependent on the ignorance or bad faith of subordinate agents. Such a one only can carry on the business of the theatre with success, and give to the English public a really good Italian opera. (pp. 176, 177)

Such is Lord Mount Edgcumbe's idea of what an Italian Opera manager ought to be: it is unquestionably just; but it is unfortunately a portrait to which we may long continue to apply the words of Juvenal—'qualem nequeo monstrare et sentio tantum'.

BELLINI

THE composer Bellini, who died in the vicinity of Paris on the 23rd of last September, is as great a loss as the musical stage, in its present circumstances, could well have sustained. His style had many beauties, but its chief characteristic was a deep and touching pathos; and his death comes unfortunately in support of a theory on which we have frequently meditated, that the faculty of pathetic musical composition, possessed in a pre-eminent degree, is the song of the swan,

> —prophetic of the doom
> Heaven gives its favourites, early death.

Need we mention Mozart and Weber? Bellini, at least, adds another name to the list of those whose music has sounded the very depths of feeling, and who have passed away while the blossom of their genius, though expanded to maturity, if judged by its actual development, could scarcely be regarded as more than a promise of the future, if judged by the ordinary relations of time.

* * *

Bellini's great force is in melody. Those who have called him an unscientific harmonist have contented themselves with the allegation and adduced no proof of it. But his harmony wants depth and variety: he rather multiplies the repetitions of the chord than gives distinct business to the several components of the score. We do not go so far as to apply to him Ritson's favourite saying: 'The only use of the harmony is to spoil the

melody'; but his harmony often smothers more than it adorns
the melody: it has neither the splendid variety of Rossini, nor
the consummate combinations of Mozart, nor the torrent of
sound of Beethoven, with its mysterious current of murmured
under-song which creeps on in such delicious and marvellous
intermixture with the vast mainstream of harmony. In all these
composers there was genius for harmony. In Bellini there is
only genius for melody. He was a melodist by nature, and a
harmonist by education. The deep and touching pathos of the
simple ballad was more accordant to his tone of mind than the
sublime and spirit-stirring volumes of sound which shake
the modern musical stage.

*   *   *

Bellini's forte was in the pathetic; but he has many charming
melodies of a more lively character, all tinged, however, in some
degree with the tone of melancholy which was natural to his
mind. There is another quality which we have remarked in his
compositions, a peculiar beauty and almost classical simplicity
in the rhythm of his compositions. We say almost classical,
because, to be perfectly so, it is essential that metre and music
should correspond syllable for note. This was indisputably the
characteristic of the ancient Greek music; and from this
acknowledged premise some writers have jumped to the conclusion that the great charm of ancient music, to which such
wonders were ascribed, must have consisted in the accurate
beating of time. They cannot imagine that music could have
been brought to much perfection without the modern liberties
of exuberant ornament. The pleasure which is derived from
mere perfect metre is familiar to all who are familiar with
classical poetry. The infinite variety of the Greek lyric metres
must have afforded some scope for variety in music; but we are
inclined to think that the perception of that kind of harmony
which resulted from the intimate correspondence of music
and metre, (adorning, in their connexion, the most perfect
lyrical poetry human genius has ever produced,) must have

caused a degree of intellectual delight, for which the complete independence of both metre and meaning, which modern music has assumed, may be but an indifferent compensation. It has occurred to us to try on one of those airs of Bellini, which we have called almost classical, the experiment of making it quite so; and by fitting it note for note to the pure metre, to which, with some difference, it naturally belongs, to try how far what it loses in musical ornament is compensated by the perception of metrical symmetry. [Examples follow.]

*   *   *

Musical critics, who hear by rule, have laboured to discredit Bellini. Fortunately reputations grow in despite of these systematical doctors. The feelings of the ordinary unsophisticated and unprejudiced hearer are always in advance of their rules; and that which has, in despite of them, been once stamped with popular favour, becomes a standard to the same class of critics in the next generation.

We have on occasions been very much amused by some of these gentry. Listening one evening with great pleasure to some beautiful modulations in one of the operas of Rossini, we were edified by a learned Theban near us, who could hear nothing but a profuse use of the diminished seventh. And we have somewhere fallen in with another variety of the same genus, who, when the whole theatre was electrified by a bold and striking effect most appropriate to the scene, could only expatiate on the harmonic atrocity of consecutive fifths, by which in a great measure the effect had been produced.

It is fitting that there should be rules in science, because they are the collected and concentrated experience of ages; but they are not to be converted into pedantic fetters to bind genius through all future time. As there is no possible sequence of sounds to which human passion does not give utterance, so there is no possible consonance or dissonance which will not find its fit place in dramatic music. Nothing was more appalling than Mrs Siddons's scream. There was no weapon in the armoury of her art which she used so sparingly; but when she did use it the occasion demanded it, and the effect was proportionate to the occasion. Rossini has taken many liberties in opposition to rules—generally because they were appropriate in their place; but sometimes, we verily believe, with mere malice prepense, to make the hair of the disciplinarians stand on end at sequences of perfect fifths or sevenths resolved by sevenths.

Akin to the pedantry of inflexible rules is that of entrenching the want of tact and feeling behind the authority of great names —saying, 'This is nought, because it is not like Mozart, or Haydn, or Beethoven, or Handel'; and thus sweeping away all modern music as with the fire of an impregnable battery. All the great names thus used had, in their own day, precisely the same sort of artillery pointed against themselves. When Beethoven was first heard of in England, it was as a madman who wrote crazy music which nobody could perform: and even where he was better known and more justly valued, all the transcendent and unrivalled dramatic talent which his *Fidelio* demonstrates, did not give him sufficient theatrical encouragement to write a second opera. Truly says Montaigne, 'Les evénements sont très maigres témoins de notre prix et capacité.' Mozart was long unknown in Paris, and has never been relished in Italy, where the anti-national use which factious pedantry has made of his name has caused him to be looked on as a sort of national enemy. Handel and Bononcini; Gluck and Piccini; Mozart and Rossini; the world of music has, in all these cases, been wide enough for both; yet it seems a necessary condition of society that there must be faction in all things.

But to be entrenched behind great names, which already bear the stamp of immortality, is an exceedingly safe position. It is an excellent *locus standi* for the fulmination of dogmas. The oracle shakes his head, and the profane take for granted that there is something in it. They give him credit for having approached the pure source, and drank from the same fountain with the great spirits with whom he seems so familiar. If we take the liberty to throw a shell into this oracular entrenchment, it is not against the great names which are misused in its construction, but against those who so misuse them, that we wish to be understood to direct it.

We stake our opinion of Bellini on the airs which we have selected, and of which our limits do not permit us to give more than the subject-melodies. But they are melodies that cannot die. They have been, are, and will be, felt and admired wherever unsophisticated perceptions sit in judgment upon them. But, as we have said, musical critics, *soi-disant par excellence*, who hear by rule, and whose chief seat of feeling is in their fingers, have so unworthily disparaged Bellini, that we have felt it a mere act of justice, as well as of gratitude, for the delight which those melodies alone (even if there were nothing else) have given us, to pay this passing tribute of honour to his memory.

FRENCH COMIC
ROMANCES

FRENCH COMIC ROMANCES

IT IS our intention, in a future Number, to give some account of the popular French novelist Paul de Kock, whose works have extended in fifteen years to the number of seventy-seven volumes; and are proceeding at the same rate with undiminished, or rather with progressively increasing, success. But before doing so, we have a few words to say of one or two of his predecessors in this branch of literature.

Paul de Kock is the legitimate successor of Pigault le Brun; and though he is, like his predecessor, *un écrivain un peu leste*, his works are, of all modern French novels, the most popular among English fashionable readers. In one respect, his writings present a striking contrast to those of his predecessor. Pigault le Brun began as a writer with the beginning of the French revolution: his successive works are impressed with the political changes of the day: they carry their era in their incidents; the actions of his heroes and heroines are interwoven with the great events that are passing around them; we live with the living witnesses and agents of the Constituent Assembly, the Legislative Assembly, the National Convention, the Executive Directory, the Consulate, and the Empire. The political and religious opinions of the author are kept always prominent; and we find him a sturdy enemy to priestcraft and tyranny throughout: with this modification, that prudence, during the Empire, restraining his politics, he gave a more undivided range to his theology. In the writings of Paul de Kock, a theological opinion is here and there slightly indicated, but a political opinion never; the era of his narratives is marked by manners only, not by political events and opinions. We are made aware that there is a government, but the only use that is made of it is to provide the hero, or one of his friends, with *une petite place dans l'adminis-tration*: there is nothing to show whether the head of it be a president, a consul, a king, or an emperor. The Sunday excursions of the Parisians—the village dances and gaieties of Sunday evening—imply a striking negation of Sir Andrew Agnew: but ecclesiastics, who cut a very conspicuous figure among the buffoons of Pigault le Brun, as they had done in French comic tales of all ages, from the Fabliaux of the twelfth century to the romances of the revolution, are never exhibited by Paul de Kock, either for good or for ill. In short, Church and State, which are always in the foreground of Pigault le Brun's pictures, are scarcely seen through the most dim perspective in those of Paul de Kock. Whether the regular succession of disappointments which have been inflicted on the friends of liberty, in the persons of Robespierre, Napoleon, the Bourbons, and Louis Philippe, has, amongst a very large class of readers, converted the bright hopes of the earlier days of the revolution into a sceptical indifference to their possible realization, is a point which we reserve for future consideration. In the meantime, we think it worth noticing, as a matter of fact, that two authors, having so many points in common, evidently not differing in opinion, and the second not less liberal than the first, present in this particular so remarkable a difference; and which is the more remarkable, because, though no preceding writers have poured forth comic romances in such abundance as these two, yet all the works of this kind which preceded the revolution—works, that is to say, illustrious in their kind—embodied opinion in a very cogent and powerful form.

In respect of presenting or embodying opinion, there are two very distinct classes of comic fictions: one in which the characters are abstractions or embodied classifications, and the implied or embodied opinions the main matter of the work; another, in which the characters are individuals, and the events and the action those of actual life—the opinions, however prominent they may be made, being merely incidental. To the first of these classes belong the fictions of Aristophanes, Petronius Arbiter, Rabelais, Swift, and Voltaire; to the latter, those of Henry Fielding, his Jonathan Wild perhaps excepted, which is a felicitous compound of both classes; for Jonathan and his gang are at once abstractions and individuals. Jonathan is at once king of the thieves and the type of an arch whig.

To the latter class belong the writings of Pigault le Brun. His heroes and heroines are all genuine flesh and blood, and invest themselves with the opinions of the time as ordinary mortals do, carrying on the while the realities of every-day life. There is often extravagance both in the characters and the actions, but it is the mere exuberance of fancy, and not like the hyperboles of Rabelais, subservient to a purpose. Rabelais, one of the wisest and most learned, as well as wittiest of men, put on the robe of the all-licensed fool, that he might, like the court-jester, convey bitter truths under the semblance of simple buffoonery.

Such was also, in a great measure, the purpose of his contemporary Bertrand de Verville, who, although he introduces *Frostibus, Lieutenant-Général de tous les diables*, apostrophizing Luther, in an exceedingly whimsical oration, as *Monsieur de l'autre monde*, was not one of the least strenuous, or least successful, supporters of the cause of the Reformation.

It would be, we think, an interesting and amusing inquiry to trace the progress of French comic fiction, in its bearing on opinion, from the twelfth century to the Revolution; and to show how much this unpretending branch of literature has, by its universal diffusion through so many ages in France, contributed to directing the stream of opinion against the mass of delusions and abuses which it was the object of those who were honest in the cause of the Reformation, and in the causes of the several changes which have succeeded it to the present time, to dissipate and destroy. If, as has frequently happened, the selfishness and dishonesty of many of the instruments has converted the triumph of a good cause into a source of greater iniquities than the triumph overthrew; if use and abuse have

9

been sometimes swept away together, and the evils of abuse have returned, while the benefits of use have been irretrievably lost; if the overthrow of religious tyranny has been made the pretext for public robbery; if the downfall of one species of state-delusion has been made the stepping-stone to the rise of a new variety of political quackery; if the quieting of civil discord has been made the basis of military despotism;* if what has been even ultimately gained in the direct object proposed, has been counterbalanced by losses in collateral matters, not sufficiently attended to in the heat of the main pursuit—(a debtor and creditor account well worthy the making out, if the requisite quantity of leisure, knowledge, and honesty could be brought to bear upon it); if the principles which were honestly pursued have been stigmatized as the necessary causes of effects which did not belong to them, and which were never contemplated by those by whom those principles were embraced; and if those who were honest in the cause have been amongst the first victims of their own triumph, perverted from its legitimate results;—we shall find, nevertheless, in the first place, that every successive triumph, however perverted in its immediate consequences, has been a step permanently gained in advance of the objects of the first authors of the Reformation—freedom of conscience and freedom of inquiry; and we shall find, in the second place, not only that comic fiction has contributed largely to this result, but that among the most illustrious authors of comic fiction are some of the most illustrious specimens of political honesty and heroic self-devotion. We are here speaking, however, solely of the authors of the highest order of comic fiction—that where limits itself, in the exposure of abuses, to turning up into full daylight their intrinsic absurdities—not that which makes ridiculous things not really so, by

---

* Lepidi atque Antonii arma in Augustum cessere: qui *cuncta, discordiis civilibus fessa*, nomine principis, sub *imperio* accepit. TACITUS, Ann. I. *Weariness of civil discord* founded the despotisms of Augustus, Cromwell, and Napoleon.

throwing over them a fool's coat which does not belong to them, or setting upon them, as honest Bottom has it, an ass's head of its own.

Ridicule, in the first case, the honest development of the ridiculous *ab intra*, is very justly denominated the test of truth: but ridicule, in the second case, the dishonest superinduction of the ridiculous *ab extra*, is the test of nothing but the knavery of the inventor. In the first case, the ridicule is never sought; it always appears, as in the comic tales of Voltaire, to force itself up obviously and spontaneously: in the second case, the most prominent feature of the exhibition is the predetermination to be caustic and comical. To writers of the latter class most truly applies the axiom—*homines derisores civitatem perdunt*. But an intense love of truth, and a clear apprehension of truth, are both essential to comic writing of the first class. An intense love of truth may exist without the faculty of detecting it; and a clear apprehension of truth may co-exist with a determination to pervert it. The union of both is rare; and still more rare is the combination of both with that peculiar 'composite of natural capacity and superinduced habit', which constitutes what is usually denominated comic genius.

We shall not lose sight of the progressive inquiry we have indicated, and shall perhaps return to it on a future occasion: but to execute it properly would require much more continuous leisure than will be readily suspected by those whose studies have not been directed into disquisitions *de rebus ludicris*. Our present purpose is much more limited.

Among the works of the successors of Rabelais, one of the most remarkable is *Le Compère Mathieu*. The design of running a tilt at predominant opinions is manifest throughout this work; but it is by no means evident what use the author, Du Laurens, proposed to make of his victory, or what doctrines he wished to exalt in the place of those he aimed to overthrow. He was himself an ecclesiastic, but his mother church was so little grateful for his labours, that she shut him up for several years in a convent of penitential friars, where he had ample leisure to meditate on the wisdom of a resolution formed by one of his own heroes, never to live in a country in which the Catholic was the dominant religion. We shall give one or two specimens of this work, which we believe has never been translated.

*   *   *

[On his final quotation Peacock comments:]

This scene is perhaps a little *outré;* but many of the main incidents of Pigault le Brun's stories are marked by a character of startling extravagance, which, to an English reader, appears at first sight out of nature; yet it is scarcely out of French nature. The movements of society in France seem to have no definite aim but the production of a *coup de théâtre.* When Louvet had denounced Robespierre, he had produced his *coup de théâtre:* his business was done, and, instead of following up his victory, he went home to supper, and sat down, *buvant frais*, with the chiefs of his party, till their festivity was interrupted by a friendly admonition to fly for their lives. When, after all the fire and fury—all the blood and thunder of the barricades— Louis Philippe and Lafayette hugged each other in a balcony, the first crying 'Henceforth the charter is a truth'; and the latter 'This is the best of republics';* there was the *coup de théâtre*—not the proposed, but the real, end of the tragi- comedy of the 'glorious three days'. There was a grand chorus and fugue on *Vive Louis Philippe!—Vive Lafayette!—Vive la Charte!*—and the curtain fell on the beautiful group in the balcony, amidst the acclamations of a crowded audience, who very soon found that this same *coup de théâtre* was the be-all and the end-all of the fruit of their magnificent exploits. The revo- lution ended like one in Pekin, where the people have the felicity of seeing Ho-Fum put over their heads in the place of Fum-Ho. The charter turned out a lie, and 'the best of republics' the beginning of the vilest and most sordid of tyrannies.

---

* There is some doubt about the words, but none about the panto- mime, of this performance.

The history of the French Revolution is a history of *coups de théâtre*, carried on with an unstudied and unconscious, but systematic and undeviating, attention to groupings, dresses, and decorations. The most overwhelming and terrific means lead to the most opposite and most farcical conclusions. *Mon Oncle Thomas*, who lays a mine under a *batterie de cuisine*, springs it with a red-hot poker, kills several dozen people, and cuts his father-in-law into halves, perpendicularly, with the lid of a fish-kettle, having no other ultimate object than that of jumping unmolested out of the window; and the author, who buries the said *Oncle* alive for thirty years in a monastic *vade in pace*, to reproduce him as the deadly foe of monks and friars, re-appearing before his relations, who had thought him dead, with a belt of Capuchins' ears in the days of the Reign of Terror, present felicitous adaptations of means to ends in comparison with the realities of the same time; or with those of the Three Glorious Days, when the end of the conflict was liberty of the press, and the final means chosen by the victors were Louis Philippe and an assemblage of vapouring deputies, who, having vanished at the first roll of the thunder of battle, emerged from their lurking-places to raise a hollow echo of the onset when the victory was won, and, after carefully abstaining from riding on the storm, to give a false direction to the tail of the whirlwind.

THE
ÉPICIER

THE ÉPICIER

WE SHALL come by-and-by to Paul de Kock, in pursuance of
the promise in the third article of our last Number; but we have
first a few more prolegomena to dispose of, and his works are so
voluminous, that we must give them an undivided notice. We
do not intend to give another version of the King of Bohemia
and his seven castles; nor to write, as Hazlitt said of Coleridge's
Friend, the everlasting prospectus of an imaginary work: and
we hope we shall not suggest the inquiry: 'Quid dignum tanto
feret hic promissor hiatu?', for there is no hiatus in the matter,
but that of an unavoidable separation in time between the beginning and the end of our subject. We shall dispose, on the
present occasion, of all that remains of our preliminaries, and
shall, on the next occasion, come without preface to the execution of our original purpose.

The remarks which we now wish to offer are pertinent to the
question which we mooted in our last Number:—Why the
writings of the most popular of modern French novelists present so striking a contrast to those of his predecessors, in being
totally divested of every trace of political opinion? The answer,
we think, is two-fold: first, there is no demand for the commodity amongst the great body of his readers; second, it does
not fall under his view as an observer of a particular class of
society.

The Greeks rejected turtle, and made a luxury of the cuttle-
fish. We make a luxury of the turtle, and make no use of the
cuttle-fish, but to turn his one bone into pounce. Accordingly,
the cuttle-fish is one of the least known to us of the creatures of

the deep, and the turtle is in the streets of London a sight of every day. Thus demand regulates supply in the most abundant productions of nature, as well as in those of human industry.

It is the same, we apprehend, with men. There was no demand for Cincinnatus in the days of Augustus. There was an old theory for Cincinnatus, but the practical tendency was for Augustus. There was no demand for Napoleon in the American revolution, nor for Washington in the French. Napoleon, in the place of Washington, could not have established a military despotism in America; nor could Washington, in the place of Napoleon, have established a democratic government in France. It was because each of them was precisely the man he was, that the practical tendency of events threw him to the surface.

So with religious observances. In an age which demands the show of sanctity testified by mortification and penance, there is no lack of a Simeon Stylites living on the top of a pillar, or of a hero like Voltaire's naked Faquir sitting *avec des clous dans le derrière pour avoir de la considération*. Comes an age which demands freedom of inquiry, the Saint and the Faquir vanish from the scene, and we have Luther demolishing the Pope with his pen, and flinging his inkstand at the head of the devil. Come the days of Church and State, and we have no hero of any sort, gymnosophist or reformer, but a host of plump well-fed parsons, who are, moreover, justices of peace and quorum, and who would commit both the Faquir and Luther, if they should show themselves within their jurisdiction, to the treadmill as rogues and vagabonds.

So with philosophy. An age which demands free inquiry, pushed without fear or compromise to its legitimate conclusions, turns up an Epicurus or a Hobbes. In one which likes to put up at an half-way house, there will be no lack of a Dugald Stewart, or a Mackintosh, to provide it with comfortable entertainment.

So with literature. Among a people disposed to think, their everyday literature will bear the impress of thought; among a people not so disposed, the absence or negation of thought will be equally conspicuous in their literature. Every variety of mind takes its station, or is ready to do so, at all times in the literary market; the public of the day stamp the currency of fashion on that which jumps with their humour. Milton would be forthcoming if he were wanted; but in our time Milton was not wanted, and Walter Scott was. We do not agree with the doctrine implied in Wordsworth's sonnet.

> Milton! thou should'st be living at this hour:
> England hath need of thee.

England would have been the better for him, if England would have attended to him, but England would not have attended to him if she had had him. There was no more market for him than for Cromwell. When Shakspeare was, Mozart and Rossini and Giulietta Grisi were not. The musical drama has struck down the legitimate. Shakspeare wrote plays, because it was the best thing he could do for himself. If he were now carrying a link before the Teatro alla Scala, he would probably limit his ambition to writing libretti for the next Gran Maestro.

French literature bore the impress of political liberty long before the Revolution, and its tendency in that line was always on the advance before that terrible political eruption. Opinion had heaved with growing strength under the pressure of custom and authority, as Typhon had tossed and tumbled many ages under Etna, before he threw up the first torrent of fire that deluged the fields of Sicily.

Pigault le Brun lived in the days of the Rights of Man, Political Justice, and Moral and Intellectual Perfectibility. Paul de Kock lives in the days of the march of mechanics, in the days of political economy, in the days of prices-current and percentages, in the days when even to dream like a democrat of the Constituent Assembly, would be held to qualify the dreamer for Bedlam; in short, in the days of the *épicier*.

Who, or what, is the *épicier?* That we shall explain presently.

It may be said that to develop opinions is not in the taste of Paul de Kock, though it was in that of Pigault le Brun. But this would be a very insufficient solution of the phenomenon. Pigault le Brun was an observer. He exhibited the play of opinion because he found it in the society he depicted. Paul de Kock is also an observer. He does not exhibit the play of opinion, because he does not find it in the society he depicts.

The case is somewhat different with a writer of romances, who draws from books and imagination, more than from actual life. With him, the development of opinion may be a matter of personal taste. But even in this case the experiment will scarcely be repeated to any extent, without a certain degree of public sympathy and encouragement. When works of fancy run out to the extent of those of Paul de Kock, or Walter Scott, we may be sure that the authors have chimed in with the predominant tastes, as well as with the predominant opinions, or negations of opinions, of a great body of readers.

Paul de Kock makes his observations on the class of the *épicier*. From this class he draws the great bulk of his characters, and the negations of opinion which characterize that class at present are faithfully reflected in the mirror which he holds up to *la nature épicière*. We shall now see what the *épicier is*.

Épicier means, as all the world doth know, grocer; but the Parisian is not exactly a counterpart of the London grocer; he is more like what, in an English country town, would be called, saving his presence, a huckster.

The *épicier* has three phases: diurnal, general, and metaphorical; the first being positive, the second negative, and the third derivative. We shall consider him first in his diurnal capacity, following the regular routine of his avocations and recreations, wherein each succeeding year rolls over the traces of its predecessor.

> Redit labor actus in orbem,
> Atque in se sua per vestigia volvitur annus.

In this capacity, M. de Balzac shall describe him for us:

> The *épicier* is the common link of all our wants, and attaches himself necessarily to all the details of human life.

'Pen, ink and paper', cries a poet. — 'Sir, there is an *épicier* at the corner of the street.'

'I am ruined!' cries a gamester. 'Powder and ball to blow my brains out.' — 'Sir, the *épicier* sells them.'

'Oh for a cigar! a real havannah: to see it consuming with a slow fire, and resolving itself into smoke: like love!' — 'The *épicier*.'

'I must give Clara an elegant breakfast. Mocha coffee, Pekoe tea; *terrine de Nérac truffée.*' — 'The *épicier*.'

Would you wake through the night? The *épicier*.

Would you sleep through the night? Still the *épicier*.

Would you have drugs to save your life, or poison to end it? Still, still, the *épicier*.

The *épicier* sells to the child his marbles, and his kite and the string that flies it; to the old invalid the eternal snuff, performing its inexhaustible and incessant circulation through snuff-box, nose, and handkerchief, making the nose of an inveterate snuff-taker an image of infinity; to the priest his wafers and tapers; slates to the schoolmaster; sugar-plums to the god-father; scented-soap to the bride; liqueur to the bridegroom; paper for the elector; fire-works for the deputy. The *épicier* has sold himself to the public, like a witch to Satan. He is the alpha and omega of all human society. You cannot travel a league, you cannot commit a crime, you cannot do a good action, you cannot make a meal, keep up an orgy, carry on a work of art, or pay court to a mistress, without having recourse to the *épicier*. He shows you the way when you inquire at his door, and follows you with his eye, with an anxious solicitude to see you go right. He is the abstract and quintessence of ever-smiling politeness. He is civilization behind a counter, society in whited-brown paper, necessity armed from head to foot; life itself distributed into drawers, bottles, bags, jugs, boxes, kegs, and cannisters. If you are abandoned by all the world except one *épicier*, you may live with him like a mouse in a cheese. When you read in golden letters *épicier du roi*, you may ask yourself with terror, 'which is most the sovereign, the *épicier* of the king, or the king of the *épicier*?'

Thus far we have seen the *épicier* in that part of his positive *phasis* which belongs to his occupation. We have yet to see him in his relaxation and recreation. But on these points Paul de Kock has so admirably portrayed him in his M. Dupont, that we shall reserve this view of him till he turns up again in his proper order.

In the mean time the reader may depict to himself a holly *bon vivant, totus teres atque rotundus,* all smooth and round, morally as well as physically, making, with a neighbour, a brace of wives and a brace of children, one of six in a *fiacre,* with a hamper wedged in the midst of them, followed by two or three more vehicles similarly stowed, to enjoy a *fête champêtre* in the environs of Paris; on his way to which we shall leave him, and look at him hereafter when he has unpacked his hamper in the Bois de Romainville.

This is the *épicier* in his diurnal functions. We must now look at him in his general or negative capacity, as a component part of the body politic, in which he stands for the representative of the whole class of dealers in whatsoever commodities, from funds to rushlights, and figures as the personification of the great clog or drag-chain on the wheels of the movement. In this his more curious and important *phasis* we shall exhibit him from a French MS. communication with which we have been favoured.

POLITICAL PHYSIOLOGY OF THE ÉPICIER

Since the Restoration the *épicier* has become the type of a class of men very widely diffused in France. There are coarse and narrow understandings which have neither the creed and feelings of the past, nor those of the future, and which maintain a fixed middle point amid the movement of ideas. This is what we call *l'esprit épicier.* Applied to literature, to the arts, to the mode of living, and manifesting itself in manner, style, and taste, by something obsolete, vulgar, and awkward, tinged with the ridiculous, this spirit has created what we call *le genre épicier.*

The *épicier* has formed his political opinions, if he has any, in the school of the *Constitutionnel.* He has not emerged from the narrow principles of the old liberalism of the Restoration. His nationality is a prejudice, without ideality, and without grandeur. He thinks himself a friend of liberty, and he sacrifices it daily by lending an unintelligent support to power. His ruling passion is the love of 'order', because he has observed that in the days of political disturbances there has been a fall of a per-centage on his operations. The apprehension of anarchy, or, to speak more correctly, the fear of diminished sales and falling prices, has made him a fanatic of 'l'ordre public'. It would be impossible to make him comprehend that the best means of consolidating public tranquillity would be to labour for the reconciliation of all the interests of society. He cannot conceive, even in moral order, any other interests than those of his trade. For him, order is a positive result which must be obtained at any price, without regard to the causes which may have produced a feverish over-excitement in any portion of society.

Abstractedly from this passion for public order, he cares little for either the monarchical form of government, or the new dynasty. In the rare instants in which he is troubled with the fancy of being witty, he makes himself merry at the expense of our rulers, their *pots-de-vin* and their *tripotages de bourse*. But while he condemns the governing body, he upholds the established order, rather than undergo the consequences of another change. He had rather keep an open account with this bad debtor, than get rid of him by settling with him at a fixed loss once for all.

It is not, therefore, any enthusiasm for the monarchical principle, it is mere self-defence that has turned him into a hero against the *émeute*, and decorated him with the cross of honour for his achievements in the campaigns of the streets. If he has still later been stimulated to the pitch of marching against the barricades of the Cloître St Méry, it was because he could not contain his rage against the republicans, who on that day, in risking their lives for the triumph of a principle, had made him lose the sale of some pounds of sugar or coffee. The next day he overflowed with stupid astonishment at the madness of those young men who had got themselves killed for an idea. It had never happened to him to have an idea in the course of his life.

Entrenched behind his counter, the *épicier* has never been carried away by the current of popular opinions: since he has seen the consequences of the Revolution resolve themselves into public calamities, he affects a superb disdain for politics. By an inconceivable confusion of ideas, he has taken effects for causes; in other words, he attributes to the ruled the faults of the rulers. He thinks himself so clear-sighted and so well-informed, that he remains deaf to all the proofs you can give him of his error.

He will not hear of the debates in the Chambers, nor of the discussions of the press, being persuaded that it is the organs of publicity which keep up perturbation in the minds of men, and, consequently, in the operations of trade. He has stereotyped the dogmas of shopkeeping indifferentism—'I never look at the papers; I have no time to read them.' 'I never meddle with politics: they do not concern me.' If by chance he tells a customer a

piece of current news, he adds immediately — 'I merely heard my
young man mention it.' In fact, his lowest shop-boys are better
informed of the course of public affairs than their master. He goes
to the coffee-house to take his *demi-tasse*, and play his game of
dominoes; but he no longer reads the newspapers, not even the
Constitutionnel, since the old journal has committed the oversight
of giving itself a few airs of independence. In short, while he is, of
all men, the most harassed by political changes, he is the one who
thinks the least about them.

Nevertheless, since the last triumph of *citizen royalty* in the
streets, political scepticism has made an irruption into the obtuse
mind of the *épicier*. He has asked himself how it can have happened
that France has been more agitated under the reign of public order,
than in that of public disturbance? There is a palpable contradic-
tion in the terms of the question, which he would try to resolve, if
it were not that above all things he anticipates with the greatest
alarm the consequences of thinking. But with all his pre-deter-
mination against inquiry, doubt having once crossed his conviction, cannot wholly pass away and leave no trace of its progress.
The time will yet arrive when the *épicier* and the republican will
meet side by side on the route of the movement.

About two years ago, at a winter evening-party in Paris, a large
part of the company had gathered round the great national lyrist
Béranger. All agreed that the monarchy was wearing itself out by
its own excesses, and consuming, in a short space, through impatience of enjoyment and mistrust of futurity, the little vitality
which remained to it. They repeated, with Napoleon, that the
time must come when republicanism would profit by the errors of
the monarchy; but they differed as to the probable distance of the
time when the republic might obtain the majority of suffrages,
and establish itself with the strongest chances of permanence.

The moderates anticipated this result as the necessary consequence of the diffusion of knowledge. Béranger, who was of that
opinion, summed it up at once, by a touch at once witty and profound. 'Believe me, gentlemen,' said he, 'you must arrive at the
republic in company with the *épicier*.'

We have here seen the *épicier* in his general *phasis*, as a great
political negation; one whom the fall of a *centime* in the price of
a pound of sugar, if he should connect it as an effect with the
cause of a 'glorious revolution', would establish, for the rest of
his days, as a dead wall in the way of an *émeute populaire*.

We may now contemplate him, in his third *phasis*, as an emblem. And in aid of this purpose, we shall draw upon an article in the *Revue Encyclopédique* for February, 1833, entitled *Études Politiques sur l'Épicier*. The article is long. We shall present so much of its essence as is needful to our purpose.

On the 29th of July, 1830, Claude Tarin (the fictitious hero of the *Studies*) poured out to Benjamin Constant the over-flowings of his enthusiasm in the cause of the three glorious days.

In the beginning of November, Claude Tarin accompanied Benjamin Constant to a sitting of the Chamber of Deputies. It was a deplorable spectacle for Claude Tarin to see the collective impersonation of false pretences, dreading either to fulfil their mission, or to betray the cause of the heroes of July, and mani-festing, in every word and gesture, the anxiety and irresolution of a rider astride on a fiery steed, fearing alike to relax or tighten the reins, and doubting whether his courser's next movement will be horizontal or perpendicular.

Benjamin Constant walked home from the assembly leaning on the arm of Tarin. In the middle of a street he stopped and said: 'My young friend, you have just seen a number of persons who have been called to exercise a good or evil influence on the progress of events. Orators, legislators, administrators, apparent chiefs of parties, have passed before you at the tribune. Yet, on my conscience, you could not see, in the faces of any of them, any such signs of an immediate and powerful authority, as you may in the face at that door on the opposite side of the street. At first sight, perhaps, he appears nothing remarkable. But look attentively. Do you not discover a singular air of prudent penetration in those little round and shaded eyes? Do not those fat cheeks of coarse and insipid air, hanging in great soft wrinkles, express an invincible pertinacity? Is not that pursed-up mouth the index of an unalterable self-satisfaction? Would it not indicate small skill in physiognomy not to recognize, in the fixedness of that equivocal smile, all the characters of im-patient desire to enjoy the present, and of indifference and in-credulity with respect to the future? Would it not be insanity to

9

suppose that any great Utopia was lodged under that low and narrow forehead, rising up into a point under that high and abundantly curled wig? Do you see nothing in those inflexible eyebrows? Are you not struck by the confident air of those arms, falling, with all their weight, at his sides, and by that massive corpulence? Can you not read a futurity about that man?'

'But,' said Claude, 'that is an *épicier*.'

'Yes, yes, it is an *épicier*. Now walk straight on, and do not look round; he has noticed that we have observed him; and the moment is not distant when his power will be more and more formidable.'

'That *épicier*!' said Claude. '*Allons,* you are a child!' said Benjamin Constant, smiling with some bitterness.

Benjamin Constant died sad and disenchanted, as every body knows.

Many, who had seen the most renowned among the defenders of public liberty successively corrupted by power, said, 'Benjamin Constant has died in time.' But Benjamin Constant had died simultaneously with the death of his last cherished illusion. He had dreamed of popular power—great, majestic, beneficent; he had seen it little, abject, ridiculous, selfish. The reality stared him in the face: he closed his eyes, and died. He who has lost his last illusion, who has used up his ideality, has nothing to do but die.

Claude Tarin remembered the last words of his deceased friend: he took a lodging in the house of the identical *épicier* pointed out by Benjamin Constant, and devoted himself to the physiological study of the *épicier*. The result of his studies was, that in the whole world of French political power—deputies, counsellors, ministers, and king—there was but one spirit, the spirit of buying and selling, on a larger or smaller scale; but regulated by no more enlightened or extensive views than those which regulated the dealings of his little landlord in coffee, treacle, and fish-sauce. He found, in short, that within the circle of the *épicier's* dealings and opinions were comprised all the aims, views, tendencies, and aspirations of the citizen-monarchy.

'It is not,' he says to some of his comrades, whom he finds seeking the means of extrication from the abyss of political despair, in which France seems to be plunged—'it is not an invisible power that governs you—it is not a prophet, not a legislator, not a tribune, not a statesman, not even a citizen—it is the *épicier!*—the palladium, the tabernacle, the *labarum* of France, the centre of all things—the alpha and omega—the elect of the great cycle of eighteen hundred and thirty!

'Enthusiasts would overthrow him. It is in vain. They might break him into atoms, they might bray him in his own mortar, they might bury him in the ruins of his counter—he would rise like the phoenix from its ashes, flourishing in portly corpulence, to reign and smile on till he shall have fulfilled his mission.

'If you think it desirable to deliver the genius of our national destiny from his actual incarnation, and to give him a more noble one, so be it: I think with you. But show me the signs of power to accomplish your purpose. Exorcize the *épicier;* trace your circle; evoke the new form which society should wear; invest it with features of moral and intellectual beauty. But in the meantime desist from evil lamentations and fruitless struggles; move not weapons that will recoil on yourselves. For the present, acknowledge yourselves conquered; bow down to the *épicier*; bend in homage to your kind.'

With this peroration terminate the *Études Politiques*.

We have now seen the *épicier* in his three phases—commercial, political and emblematical; and we can now easily understand that the grand incarnation of *l'esprit épicier*, the citizen-king, sits safe on his throne, because the *épicier* is not now, as in 1790, an *enfant de la patrie* singing the Marseillois hymn, or at least listening approvingly to those who sang it; but a *gendarme* determined to uphold whatever is uppermost, provided it will let him deal without molestation; but because he likes or admires what is uppermost, or would cross the street to fetch it back if it were once fairly turned out, but because he has had sufficient

experience of change of masters to desire to change no more. He
remembers the sayings and doings of 1789; he has asked himself what good he and his class have gained by any past political
change, which, placed as a solid gain in one scale, would
counterbalance his loss by a single fall of a denier in the price
of any one of his commodities, when his *boutique* was stored, on
the other? and he has answered—*Nil*. In politics he discusses
nothing, aims at nothing, anticipates nothing. He acquiesces
and maintains. He is the great *vis inertiæ* that presses down
anarchy, and upholds the colossal mass of brute physical force,
embodied in military power, which supports the existing order
of things. He is the broad-backed tortoise that stands upon
chaos, and carries the elephant that carries the world—the
world of France: on which, like Eblis in his hall, sits enthroned
le grand épicier—the Citizen-King: the grand master of the
order of *L'Épicerie*: the king of the sugar-market, and the auto-
crat of the stock-exchange: the embodied spirit of the age, and
of all the ages of all the exchanges of the world—brokerages,
agiotages, mortgages, averages, and per-centages: the reverse of
'no waiter, but a knight templar', being in truth no knight, but
an *épicier*.

But the *épicier*—passive substratum as he is—is, like the great
passive substratum, his mother earth, 'one shape of many
names',* as Æschylus has it, diffusing his own life through all
that lives above him. The influence of his spirit is everywhere
positive and predominant. The *épicier* votes—the *épicier* elects;
the *épicier* does not discuss, but the *épicier* decides, and the
épicier administers. The *épicier* rules the court and the camp,
the bourse and the bureau; the *épicier* wields the sword of the
national guard, and the sceptre of the citizen-king. In short, the
whole existing political system of France is one *grande boutique
d'épicerie*.

Thus there is in France a mass of fiery youth tending per-
petually to a republic; a government, no matter how called, or

---

* Πολλῶν ὀνομάτων μορφὴ μία.

on what principles and professions originally based, repressing this tendency by force; the progressive increase of the opposite pressures, every now and then generating an explosion; and the *épicier*, with his confirmed habit of order, satisfied with any form of government under which he may buy and sell in peace, bringing the vast bulk of his own dead weight to the upholding of any mode of authority which accident has made uppermost at the end of the turmoil, and which seems to him likely to keep prices looking up, and to throw no cloud over his Sunday enjoyment of the suburban picturesque.

We are now, we think, sufficiently deep in the *physiologie de l'épicier* to understand why writings, founded mainly on observation of this class of society, do not meddle with political opinions, or beat time in any way to the march of the movement.

Since writing the above, we have received and read Paul de Kock's last novel, *Ni Jamais, ni Toujours*, in which, for the first time, we find an indication, but a very slight one, of political opinion: it amounts to nothing more than an expression of regret that destruction has been so much more vigorous than construction: a position, however, which, carried out into its practical, or rather into its non-practical results, will be found to furnish the basis of *la philosophie épicière*.

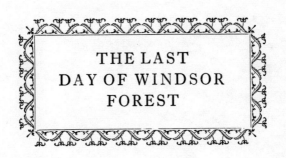

THE LAST
DAY OF WINDSOR
FOREST

THE LAST DAY OF WINDSOR FOREST

MANY of my younger, and some of my maturer years, were passed on the borders of Windsor Forest. I was early given to long walks and rural explorations, and there was scarcely a spot of the Park or the Forest, with which I was not intimately acquainted. There were two very different scenes, to which I was especially attached: Virginia Water, and a dell near Winkfield Plain.

The bank of Virginia Water, on which the public enter from the Wheatsheaf Inn, is bordered, between the cascade to the left and the iron gates to the right, by groves of trees, which, with the exception of a few old ones near the water, have grown up within my memory. They were planted by George the Third, and the entire space was called the King's Plantation. Perhaps they were more beautiful in an earlier stage than they are now: or I may so think and feel, through the general preference of the past to the present, which seems inseparable from old age. In my first acquaintance with the place, and for some years subsequently, sitting in the large upper room of the Inn, I could look on the cascade and the expanse of the lake, which have long been masked by trees.

Virginia Water was always open to the public, through the Wheatsheaf Inn, except during the Regency and reign of George the Fourth, who not only shut up the grounds, but enclosed them, where they were open to a road, with higher fences than even the outside passengers of stage-coaches could look over, that he might be invisible in his punt, while fishing on the lake. William the Fourth lowered the fences, and re-opened the old access.

While George the Third was king, Virginia Water was a very

solitary place. I have been there day after day, without seeing another visitor. Now it has many visitors. It is a source of great enjoyment to many, though no longer suitable to *Les Rêveries d'un Promeneur Solitaire*.

A still more solitary spot, which had especial charms for me, was the deep forest dell already mentioned, on the borders of Winkfield Plain. This dell, I think, had the name of the Bourne, but I always called it the Dingle. In the bottom was a water-course, which was a stream only in times of continuous rain. Old trees clothed it on both sides to the summit, and it was a favourite resort of deer. I was a witness of their banishment from their forest-haunts. The dell itself remained some time unchanged: but I have not seen it since 1815, when I frequently visited it in company with Shelley, during his residence at Bishopgate, on the eastern side of the Park. I do not know what changes it may have since undergone. Not much, perhaps, being now a portion of the Park. But many portions of the Park and its vicinity, as well as of the immediate neighbourhood of Windsor, which were then open to the public, have ceased to be so, and such may be the case with this. I have never ventured to ascertain the point. In all the portions of the old forest, which were distributed in private allotments, I know what to expect. I shrink from the ghosts of my old associations in scenery, and never, if I can help it, revisit an enclosed locality, with which I have been familiar in its openness.

Wordsworth would not visit Yarrow, because he feared to disappoint his imagination:

> Be Yarrow stream unseen, unknown!
>   It must, or we shall rue it:
> We have a vision of our own,
>   Ah! why should we undo it?
> The treasured dreams of times long past,
>   We'll keep them, winsome Marrow!
> For when we're there, although 'tis fair,
>   'Twill be another Yarrow.*

---

* *Yarrow Unvisited.*

Yet, when he afterwards visited it, though it was not what he had dreamed, he still found it beautiful, and rejoiced in having seen it:

> The vapours linger round the heights:
>   They melt, and soon must vanish:
> One hour is theirs, nor more is mine:
>   Sad thought, which I would banish,
> But that I know, where'er I go,
>   Thy genuine image, Yarrow!
> Will dwell with me, to heighten joy,
>   And cheer my mind in sorrow.*

He found compensation in the reality, for the difference of the imagined scene: but there is no such compensation for the disappointments of memory: and when—in the place of scenes of youth, where we have wandered under antique trees, through groves and glades, through bushes and underwood, among fern, and foxglove, and bounding deer; where, perhaps, every 'minutest circumstance of place'† has been not only 'as a friend' in itself, but has recalled some association of early friendship, or youthful love—we can only pass between high fences along dusty roads, I think it best to avoid the sight of the reality, and to make the best of cherishing at a distance

> The memory of what has been,
> And never more will be.‡

---

* *Yarrow Visited.*

†   But thou hast viewed
These scenes, like one who passes through a land,
Where his heart is not. I, my friend, long time
Had sojourned there; and I am one who form
With each minutest circumstance of place
Acquaintance, and the unfrequented field,
Where many a day I walk in solitude,
Is as a friend to me.

Southey's *Epistle to Amos Cottle*, prefixed to the latter's *Icelandic Poetry*. It is strange, that this Epistle was not included in Southey's collected works. It is one of the best of his minor poems, and would alone suffice to show, that he had 'looked on nature with a poet's eye.'

‡ Wordsworth.

I do not express, or imply, any opinion on the general utility of enclosures. For the most part, they illustrate the scriptural maxim: 'To him that hath much, much shall be given; and from him that hath little shall be taken away, even the little he hath.' They are, like most events in this world, 'Good to some, bad to others, and indifferent to the majority.' They are good to the land-owner, who gets an addition to his land: they are bad to the poor parishioner, who loses his rights of common: they are bad to the lover of rural walks, for whom footpaths are annihilated: they are bad to those, for whom the scenes of their youth are blotted from the face of the world. These last are of no account in ledger balances, which profess to demonstrate that the loss of the poor is more than counterbalanced by the gain of the rich; that the aggregate gain is the gain of the community; and that all matters of taste and feeling are fitly represented by a cypher. So be it.

George the Fourth's exclusions and high fences had not, however, effectually secured to him the secrecy he desired. On an eminence outside of the royal grounds, stood, and still stands, in the midst of a pine-grove, a tower, which from its form was commonly called the Clock-case. This tower, and the land round it, had been sold for a small sum, as a lot in a sale of Crown Lands. The tower was in two or three stories, and was inhabited by a poor family, who had a telescope, supplied, most probably, by the new proprietor, on the platform of the roof, which rose high above the trees, and commanded an extensive view of the lake. This tower and its grounds became a place of great resort for pic-nic parties, and visitors of all kinds, who kept up a perpetual succession at the telescope, while the Royal Angler and his fair companion were fishing. This became an intolerable nuisance to the would-be recluse. He set on foot a negociation for re-purchasing the Clock-case. The sum demanded was many times the multiple of the purchase-money. The demand was for some time resisted, but the proprietor was inflexible. The sum required was paid, the property reverted to the Crown, and the public were shut out from the

Clock-case and its territory. When William the Fourth succeeded, this story was told to him, and he said: 'A good place for a view, is it? I will put an old couple into it, and give them a telescope': which was done without loss of time. I saw and conversed with this old couple, and looked through their telescope.

About the same time, William the Fourth was sitting one Sunday evening in a window of Windsor Castle, when the terrace was thronged with people.

A heavy rain came on, and the people ran in all directions. He said to some one near him: 'This is the strangest thing I ever saw: so many English people, without an umbrella among them.' He was told that, by order of his late Majesty, umbrellas were prohibited on the terrace. 'Then,' he said, 'let the prohibition be immediately withdrawn.'

In the early days of his reign, he was fond of walking about, not only in Windsor, but in London. It pleased him to be among the people. In one of his walks, he noticed, in Windsor Little Park, a board with an inscription, by which all persons were 'ordered' to keep the footpath. He desired that 'requested' might be substituted. He was told, that 'requested' would not be attended to. He said: 'If they will not attend to "requested" that is their affair: I will not have "ordered".'

A most good-natured, kind-hearted gentleman was William the Fourth: but to record the many instances of good feeling in his sayings and doings, which came within my knowledge, would be foreign to the purpose of the present paper.

The Act for the enclosure of Windsor Forest contained the following clause:

WINDSOR FOREST.

53rd George III. Cap. 158.

LXIV.—And be it further enacted, That from and after the first day of July one thousand eight hundred and fourteen, all and singular the Lands, Tenements and Hereditaments within the said respective Parishes and Liberties (save and except such Parts thereof respectively as are now or shall or may become vested in

His Majesty, or any Person or Persons in Trust for Him by virtue
hereof) shall be, and the same is and are hereby disafforested to all
Intents and Purposes whatsoever; and that from thenceforth no
Person or Persons shall be questioned or liable to any Pain, Penalty
or Punishment for hunting, coursing, killing, destroying or taking
any Deer whatsoever within the same, save and except within such
Part or Parts thereof (if any) as shall be enclosed with Pales and
kept for a Park or Parks by the Owners, Lessees, or Tenants
thereof.

There can be little doubt, that the exception in favour of the
Crown was intended to apply to all the provisions of the clause:
but it was held by Counsel learned in the law, that it applied to
the first half only, and that, after the specified day, it was lawful
to kill deer in any portion of the old forest, not enclosed with
pales, whether such portion had, or had not, been vested in the
Crown. The Crown allotment had been left as it was.

Armed with this opinion, a farmer of Water Oakley, whose
real I have forgotten in his assumed name, calling himself Robin
Hood, and taking with him two of his men, whom he called
Scarlet and Little John, sallied forth daily into the forest to kill
the king's deer, and returned home every evening, loaded with
spoil.

Lord Harcourt, who was then Deputy Ranger of the Forest,
and discharged all the duties of superintendence (for the
Ranger, who was a Royal Highness, of course did nothing),
went forth also, as the representative of Majesty, to put down
these audacious trespassers. In my forest-rambles, I was a witness to some of their altercations: Lord Harcourt threatening to
ruin Robin Hood by process in the Court of Exchequer; Robin
Hood setting him at defiance, flourishing the Act of Parliament,
and saying: 'My Lord, if you don't know how to make Acts of
Parliament, I'll teach you.'

One day, I was walking towards the Dingle, when I met a
man with a gun, who asked me, if I had seen Robin Hood? I
said, I had just seen him at a little distance, in discussion with
Lord Harcourt, who was on horseback, Robin Hood being on
foot. He asked me to point out the direction, which I did; and

in return I asked him, Who he might be? He told me, he was Scarlet. He was a pleasant-looking man, and seemed as merry as his original: like one in high enjoyment of sport.

This went on some time. The law was not brought to bear on Robin Hood, and it was finally determined to settle the matter, by driving the deer out of the forest into the Park. Two regiments of cavalry were employed for this purpose, which was kept as secret as possible, for a concourse of people would have been a serious impediment to the operation. I received intelligence of it from a friend at court, who pointed out to me a good position, from which to view the close of the proceedings.

My position was on a rising ground, covered with trees, and overlooking an extensive glade. The park was on my left hand: the main part of the forest on the right and before me. A wide extent of the park paling had been removed, and rope fencing had been carried to a great length, at oblique angles from the opening. It was a clear calm sunny day, and for a time there was profound silence. This was first broken by the faint sound of bugles, answering each other's signals from remote points in the distance: drawing nearer by degrees, and growing progressively loud. Then came two or three staggling deer, bounding from the trees, and flying through the opening of the park pales. Then came greater numbers, and ultimately congregated herds: the beatings of their multitudinous feet mingled with the trampling of the yet unseen horses, and the full sounds of the bugles. Last appeared the cavalry, issuing from the wood, and ranging themselves in a semi-circle, from horn to horn of the rope fencing. The open space was filled with deer, terrified by the chase, confused by their own numbers, and rushing in all directions: the greater part through the park opening: many trying to leap the rope fencing, in which a few were hurt, and one or two succeeded: escaping to their old haunts, most probably to furnish Robin Hood with his last venison feast. By degrees, the mass grew thinner: at last, all had disappeared: the rope fencing shut up the park for the night: the cavalry rode off towards Windsor: and all again was silent.

This was, without any exception, the most beautiful sight I ever witnessed: but I saw it with deep regret: for, with the expulsion of the deer, the life of the old scenes was gone, and I have always looked back on that day, as the last day of Windsor Forest.